Gordon Wedson
Ps. 159

THE COLLEGE
TRAP

Web-based Financial Guide
for Students and Parents

Gordon H. Wadsworth

Library of Congress Control Number: 2006911238

Wadsworth, Gordon H.
The College Trap: Web-based Financial Guide for Students and Parents / Gordon H. Wadsworth
I. Title

ISBN-13: 978-0-9659682-1-8

PUBLISHER'S NOTE:
In some cases, names of people and places have been altered to protect their privacy. All programs, grants and scholarships noted within are subject to change and shall not be the responsibility of the publisher and/or the copyright owner. This publication is not intended to provide professional accounting or financial advice. For expert financial counseling, please contact a Certified Financial Planner in your community.

Dedication

*To my friends and financial advisors
who helped make this publication possible,
and to my wife Janet for her encouragement, devotion
and long hours perusing this manuscript.*

Table of Contents

NOTE: ALL INTERNET LINKS IN **TheCollegeTrap** ARE UNDERLINED.
TO ACTIVATE THE WEB LINKS, GO TO WWW.THECOLLEGETRAP.INFO

Preface

During the past 15 years a major change has taken place in the academic world. Because of the ease with which students can now acquire credit cards, leased automobiles and government loans, the burden of paying for college has shifted from the parents to the student. With scores of families already weighted down by multiple car payments, heavy credit card debt, the shrinking dollar and rising fuel costs, some parents feel the change couldn't have come at a more appropriate time.

Nationally known pastor and author, Andy Stanley, wrote, "Many times I hear of young people who want to serve the Lord in ministry but are financially enslaved because of debt." Students today are beginning to ask questions: Is it worth graduating from college with $20,000 or $30,000 or even $60,000 in debt? Will I really end up in financial bondage for years? Why is it that tuition increases far exceed the overall inflation rate? And finally, do I really need a college education to advance in this world? We will endeavor to answer these questions and more in *TheCollegeTrap.*

A college diploma can be one of the most challenging 4 or 5 years in anyone's life, but well worth the investment of time, money and emotion. The key is to remain free of the debt that's plaguing the country's graduating seniors. Yet, to do so requires discipline as well as creative planning. Advanced planning may include the military or attending a local community college prior to transferring to a recognized

4-year institution, or even attending college online. We'll explore the options and help you make wise decisions as you move forward.

A learned author and radio personality, Larry Burkett, once told a caller to his national broadcast, "It's not how much money you have but how you manage what you have." Based on that premise, we have an expanded money management chapter plus budget worksheets found in Appendix Two.

You can earn a college diploma by carefully managing your every resource and avoiding the college trap that's packed with government loans.

G. W.

Introduction

Students in Financial Bondage

Difficult Times Ahead

In an article written for an online Focus on the Family magazine, Heather Koerner recently described the student loans entrapping law school graduate Ashley. Although thrilled to receive her sought-after law degree, Ashley's problem is the debt that hangs on and never seems to go away. In fact, at $500 per month, it will take her years to pay off the loans.

Now in her early 30's, Ashley hopes to someday start a family. "I'd like to stay home with my kids or at least work part-time. I hope that's possible," said Ashley. She's overwhelmed realizing that she may be a grandmother before she is completely rid of her student loans.

"According to most experts, for student loan debt to stay 'manageable' the monthly payment cannot exceed 8 percent of the monthly income," Koerner says. "So to cover that $500, Ashley needs to earn at least $6,250 a month or $75,000 a year." That's extremely difficult if you're a stay-at-home mom working only part-time.

John and Lisa found themselves deep in debt after college graduation. They put the blame on the ease of acquiring credit cards. "My husband and I ended up with a total of 14 credit cards while we were college students," the 25-year-old woman told the counselor. "Then after we got married and had two children, our medical bills started adding up until we finally filed bankruptcy." Lisa acknowledged receiving a gift each time she signed up for a new credit card, but then added, "The free T-shirt is not worth it."

In a recent phone call asking for help with student loans, Shelly tearfully poured out her story of financial entrapment. Shelly and her husband have 3 small children, but they also have over $40,000 in student loans. Unable to make regular payments, the loans are all in default. Referring to the government insisting on repayment, she cried, "Why don't they understand?"

Some months ago there was a phone call from a man who didn't identify himself at first, but as the conversation moved ahead he asserted, "I've been paying on my student loan for years. I still owe $39,000. It never seems to go down. To make it even worse, I am a dentist with full time staff assisting me. Because my student loan is in default, I cannot buy a house. I cannot buy a car. I drive an old $600 car and park it in the back so none of my patients will see it. I don't know what to do."

Currently, over $40 billion in student loan debt has forced many former students into financial bondage and even bankruptcy. At the same time the student loan rate has soared, the personal savings rate in America has declined nationwide to almost $70 billion.

Why Another Book?

This is not just another book about financial assistance. *TheCollegeTrap* is a book totally committed to helping you avoid the financial bondage that is plaguing the nation's graduating seniors. Our research team continually monitors the college financial aid world to provide you the latest information to help you graduate without entrapment.

A classic student loan snare is found in an advertisement from a national student loan operator. The ad features three $10,000 student loan examples with convenient 20 to 24-year paybacks, each one worse than the other. The plans include an interest-only and even a deferred payback plan for the student still in college. The results: For the initial $10,000 loan, students are required to pay back between $21,398 and $29,860, or between 114 percent and 299 percent of the original loan amount.

TheCollegeTrap will walk you through a simple step-by-step application process and show you ways to qualify for federal and state grants and service cancelable loans. We'll also explain how the Expected Family Contribution is calculated and why some students qualify for scholarships and grants and other students qualify only for those dreaded student loans.

We'll easily debunk the myth about the "lost and unused scholarships" and reveal where you can find bona fide college scholarships and how to qualify for federal and state grants.

If you're just returning to college or would prefer to attend college on your computer, we'll update you on the latest information regarding distance education as well as which colleges and universities are now offering online degrees.

The government has many programs for students who have already graduated to rid themselves of their heavy student loans. Included in **TheCollegeTrap** are ways to cancel student debt via multiple service cancelable loan options, government employment after graduation, or pro-college military options.

Each year we learn that more students are defaulting on their student loans. Yet, many still believe the easiest way to finance their education is to borrow from the government. Accepting a Stafford Loan can be your worst nightmare. We'll reveal the *true cost*. Once you know the real cost, you might think twice before accepting the high interest loan.

The Government's Effect on Tuition

One of the biggest concerns for parents today is which college will be the best for their student. Of equal or greater importance is the overall cost, especially since less than 25% of college students graduate in four years.

Next to buying a home, paying for college can be the greatest financial challenge you'll ever face. A home mortgage can be amortized (payments spread out) over three decades, whereas college tuition must be paid every quarter or semester. There are many factors involved in selecting a college; finances often dictate the final choice.

The cost factor was less of a concern before the mid-1980s. Prior to that time, families were able to keep more of their earned income, surrendering less to the government for income taxes, Social Security and Medicare. In addition, state schools were heavily subsidized in the past, allowing them to offer a college education for a minimum investment.

Equally significant, the federal government had not yet entered the student loan business. The federal government's involvement has only helped to accelerate the rise in tuition costs. Third-party lenders such as banks, state governments, credit unions, and insurance companies funded the original Stafford Loans as part of the Federal Family Education Loan Program (FFELP), with the federal government merely acting as the guarantor. Once the federal government decided to get involved in the direct lending pandemonium in the mid-1990s, many of the banks dropped out.

Student loan rates change every July 1st. With the increased interest rates for both the Federal Stafford Loan and the Parent Loan for Undergraduate Students (PLUS), many third-party lenders are again offering student loans at the higher interest rates set by the government. Colleges and universities can choose whether to offer student loans under the Federal Family Education Loan Program or the Direct Loan Program.

Why Tuition Continues to Rise

College tuitions soar each year, advancing far in excess of the inflation rate. One reason for this continual rise is directly related to the lack of state subsidies. Funds once set aside for higher education are now being used for rising Medicaid costs, construction of new detention facilities, and repairing streets and highways.

Many schools have also been forced to increase tuition fees due to increasing overhead costs. Fuel and labor costs continue to rise. Many older college buildings need to be renovated or replaced. The demand for expanded libraries and new research and computer labs is at an all-time high. Some schools also need additional security measures.

Perhaps the main reason tuition continues to rise is the change made in 1992 regarding the Stafford Loan. When Uncle Sam opened the floodgates to government-backed student loans without parent income restrictions, colleges welcomed the news with open arms. The sudden injection of millions of additional aid dollars only furthered tuition increases. Add the government's continued promotion of the Stafford Loan as a low-cost program, and you have the formula for hyperinflationary costs.

Once the federal government made it exceptionally easy for students to borrow massive amounts of money, colleges followed the lead by increasing their tuition rates. This combination has led to record-level borrowing. Today the average undergraduate student loan debt is nearing $20,000. Those who go on to graduate school often end up with an additional $30,000. Law and medical students report an average accumulated debt from all years (undergraduate and graduate study) of $91,700.

The unsubsidized Stafford Loan is basically an *entitlement* program open to all families regardless of income and net worth. The interest accrues the entire time a student is in school. Even though it's possible to pay the interest every quarter, most students choose to let it accumulate until they graduate. This only furthers the debt dilemma.

When the Health Education Assistance Loan program was phased out, the US Department of Education increased the overall loan limit on unsubsidized Stafford Loans for those studying medicine, dentistry, podiatry, optometry, osteopathy, veterinary medicine, pharmacy, and others to $189,125, less any subsidized loans from their undergraduate study. A student earning a master's degree is permitted to borrow up to $138,500 from the federal government without any credit qualifications or assets.

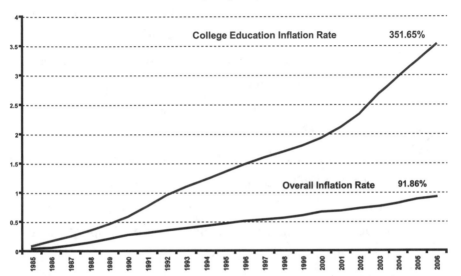

You may wonder if the college is at fault when students end up in financial bondage after four years of advanced schooling. Understandably, the colleges deny any wrong doing and place the blame on the carefree lifestyle that many college students enjoy. Yet, the fact remains that college tuition increases have soared, seemingly out of control.

Reporting in a recent article on Foxnews.com, Maja Tarateta writes, "While endowments are growing and more universities are engaging in billion-dollar fund-raising campaigns, the cost of tuition for students continues to increase."

Based on statistical research from Tim McMahon at InflationData. com, the overall inflation rate since 1986 increased 91.86%, which is why we pay nearly double for everything we buy. On the other hand, during the same time period, tuition increased a whopping 351.65%.

For example, if the cost of college tuition was $10,000 in 1986, it would now cost the same student over $43,000 or almost 2½ times the inflation rate.

As of this writing, only a handful of prominent universities have chosen to reduce the excessive loan debt that students carry by drawing upon their extensive endowment funds. Indeed, those schools should be applauded for their decision, and benefactors should be encouraged to give even more to their alma mater based on the forward thinking of the college's executive board.

The government is overly lenient in handing out taxpayer money for student loans, but highly demanding when it comes to student loan repayment. Much like an income tax debt owed to the Internal Revenue Service, a student loan cannot be canceled via a bankruptcy except in very rare cases as determined by the court.

Remaining debt free in college isn't easy, but it is possible. It requires a great deal of planning, perseverance and commitment. College students today must shoulder the overall responsibility for their education and maintain a workable spending plan, and essentially become reliable money managers.

Chapter I

How to Apply

Which Forms to Use

Types of financial aid are highly diverse. They are composed of a mosaic of public, private, and institutional sources. Applying for financial aid is not difficult. It is, however, a highly structured procedure and one you must follow carefully. If you make errors or do not file the proper forms on time, you may get your money late or lose it altogether.

The first thing you need to know is which financial aid application the college wants. Some private schools will not consider any government aid, refusing all forms of federal grants and student loans. The schools with this philosophy maintain their independence from Washington, thus eliminating some of the programs that have plagued other institutions. These schools make their beliefs well known. They have deep convictions that Uncle Sam should be a distant relative when it comes to any kind of handout. As a result, the schools provide their own financial aid forms.

Most colleges and universities want all incoming students to file the federal government's Free Application for Federal Student Aid (FAFSA) after January 1st of the award year. This applies to students whether home schooled or schooled in a private or public school. The preprinted

FAFSA is available from college financial aid offices and high school guidance counselors. It is similar to working on federal taxes using the government's 1040 form. Both you and your parents must include:

> *File the FAFSA after January first of the award year.*

- Adjusted gross income
- Assets
- Federal taxes paid
- The number of members in your family
- The number attending college at least part-time
- The age of your older parent

This process, known as *need-analysis*, is the means for establishing your financial need. Some people feel the information requested by the government is an invasion of their privacy and refuse to apply for any federal assistance.

A student whose parents are divorced or separated needs only to indicate the income of the parent with whom he or she resides at least 51percent of the time. If that parent remarries, the student must provide the stepparent's income even if the stepparent provides no financial assistance or support.

Once you complete the FAFSA, mail the form to the central processing center. Two to 3 weeks later you will receive a copy of the Student Aid Report (SAR). The report reveals the Expected Family Contribution (EFC), or the amount you and your parents are expected to pay for college. The report also indicates your eligibility for a Federal Pell Grant or the Supplemental Educational Opportunity Grant (SEOG).

If you want to know your EFC before completing the FAFSA form, we recommend the free online calculator at Family Contribution.

You can log into the FAFSA website to complete the form online.

The FAFSA site will give you a PIN number to speed up the process. You need only one application no matter how many colleges receive your financial information.

Many private schools want information not requested on the federal application including the value of your family's residence or farm. In addition to the federal form, these institutions ask you to complete a Financial Aid Profile® from the College Scholarship Service, the financial arm of the College Board. The cost is $5 to register plus $18 for each school that receives your information. To order, click here

Expected Family Contribution Examined

After the colleges receive a copy of your Student Aid Report from the central processing center, the financial aid staff will analyze your information to decide which type of financial aid package to offer. A financial aid package is unique to each student. Your personal financial need may be met by a combination of grants, scholarships, loans, and a work-study program. Because all student financial aid is directly related to the EFC, a student with a superior national test score plus an outstanding grade point average may be offered a large percentage of scholarships. Another student may find his or her financial aid package packed with government loans.

> *All financial aid is directly related to the Expected Family Contribution.*

Private institutions may, at their discretion, choose which report to use in their financial analysis. For a highly desirable student, the school may use the EFC generated by the federal form. For another student, the school may use the Profile® form, which may increase the family's contribution by adding home assets to the formula and reducing the amount of institutional aid. While nearly all colleges and universities can and do negotiate tuition and financial aid, most parents are at a huge disadvantage when it comes to negotiating their own student's education. One firm that has had good success in saving students money and even negotiating with colleges is College Assistance Plus at CAPlus.

The way the government determines the EFC does not always reflect your family's ability to pay for college nor your debt load and overall need. The government considers neither family medical bills nor secondary tuition fees. How a student's family meets the need determines how much debt the student will have at graduation.

The government's definition of need is the difference between the EFC and the actual cost of attendance. For example, if your expected contribution is $4,500, you may have no financial need. The reason: a local community college may cost around $4,000 a year. If the EFC is set at $4,500, the government expects that your family has the available funds and will be able to pay the entire cost.

If you plan to attend a school where the tuition, room, board and books cost approximately $17,000, the difference of $12,500 is then determined to be your financial need ($17,000 less the $4,500 EFC).

Most are surprised at how much personal income and assets affect the EFC. Ideally, grandparents who want to help with college finances should give the money to the student's parents. (The IRS allows gifts of $12,000 per year to children without any tax penalty.) An even better way may be for grandparents to wait until after graduation to help pay off some of the student loans.

Likewise, parents should not borrow from a retirement account since those assets are shielded from the needs analysis formula, as are tax-deferred annuities and whole life policies.

1. The government expects 50 percent of a student's earnings over $2,200 to be added to the EFC.

2. The government expects 35 percent of all assets held in a student's name to be used each year for tuition and other college expenses. It may be wise to utilize the student's assets before filling out the FAFSA. For example, students could use their savings to pay for an automobile, dorm refrigerator, microwave, DVD recorder, computer or even new computer software, none of which will be considered in the needs analysis formula.

3. Only 5.65 percent of assets held in the parent's name count towards the EFC. Families with large cash assets may want to consider reducing their cash assets prior to filling out the FAFSA by paying off credit card debt, automobile loans, or even a home mortgage. Parents may also elect to postpone bonuses or any capital gains while you are in college, as both will reduce the amount of your financial assistance.

College Award Letter

During the spring and summer months, colleges send students a notification of financial aid, often called the award letter. This letter explains the kind of aid the college is offering a student for the following academic year. For recruiting purposes, some schools may send a preliminary financial aid package in the fall of the student's senior year in high school, pending verification of the Student Aid Report.

If the amount and type of financial aid shown in your award letter is unsatisfactory, you may appeal the decision by meeting with the *head* of the financial aid department where you have been accepted. Not everyone receives special considerations, but enough do to warrant the time and effort. Student financial aid should never be negotiated in letters or over the phone.

The financial aid administrator has extensive authority. With proper documentation, the administrator may adjust the components that determine the EFC at his or her discretion. You must be able to document special circumstances before the school's financial aid administrator can make a professional judgment. The final decision is left to the administrator. The decision may not be appealed to the US Department of Education.

> *Student financial aid should never be negotiated in letters or over the phone.*

Independent Status

Certain students are considered independent. They must include only their own income on the federal application form. This generally lowers the EFC and increases the chances for a Pell Grant. There are very specific rules governing independent status. Unless students meet the qualifications below, they are considered dependent, even if they don't live with their parents nor receive financial support. To be classified as independent, a student must meet one of the following requirements:

a. Be 24 years of age by December 31

b. An orphan or ward of the court

c. A veteran of the Armed Services

d. A professional or graduate student

e. Married with or without dependents

f. Have dependents other than a spouse

g. Be judged independent by Administrator

Self-supporting students who do not meet any of the qualifications are encouraged to appeal directly to the financial aid administrator at the college.

Private Colleges

Applying to a private or Christian college is the same as applying to any other college. Applying for financial aid is also the same. Applicants are required to file the FAFSA form, the Profile®, or the school's own financial aid form.

Many students at a Christian college will have an opportunity to study abroad. In fact, more than half of the schools affiliated with the Coalition for Christian Colleges and Universities provide students with an international study term and Christian outreach. Reportedly, 85 percent of the students at Goshen College in Indiana spend thirteen weeks in a foreign country learning the language and customs while living with a host family.

Christian schools today have competitive financial aid programs. Numerous students at Toccoa Falls College in Northeast Georgia reduce their education costs by assisting local school districts. Through the America Reads Program, students earn up to $2,500 per year tutoring kindergarten through third grade children in reading and math. Toccoa Falls offers a work credit program where the earned income may be used for tuition, books or related expenses. For additional information, call 800-868-3257 or go to Toccoa Falls College. To apply for financial aid at Toccoa Fall, parents and students use the FAFSA form.

Pensacola Christian College in Florida at PCCI has declined federal student aid to remain free of government interference. Yet, an extensive array of student financial aid is available. Nearly 50 percent of the 4,000 students on campus pay their own college expenses through the school's work assistance program. Students may earn up to $2,800 per year to help offset the school's affordable tuition fees. For more information, call 800-PCC-INFO. To apply for assistance, request the college's own financial aid application.

Nestled between the ocean and the mountains overlooking Santa Barbara, California, Westmont College offers an interest-free loan to California high school graduates based on the information gathered on the FAFSA form. In addition to the Pell Grant, the service cancelable Perkins Loan and the Federal Work-Study program, Westmont College also offers incoming students institutional grants and scholarships based on academic achievement. Sixty percent of all students receive student financial aid that is not repayable. For more information on student financial aid, log on Westmont or call 800-777-9011.

Taylor University in Indiana provides eligible students federal grants. They also participate in the Federal Work-Study program in which students may earn $1,800 or more per year. In addition to a Christian Leadership Scholarship worth 25 percent of tuition, students may be eligible to receive a Church Matching Grant of $750 per year for any funds contributed from a church or Para-church organization. Students in the top 10 percent of their high school class may be eligible for the University's President's Scholarship worth 20 percent of tuition and renewable annually. Those who rank in the top 15 percent may qualify for Taylor University's Dean's Scholarship for 15 percent of tuition. Call 765-998-5206 for more information. To be considered for financial aid, students need to complete the FAFSA form.

Palm Beach Atlantic College on Florida's East coast offers institutional scholarships, including those based on church attendance and activities. Florida residents may qualify for a Limited Access Grant and the Resident Grant in addition to the Pell Grant. By completing the Free Application for Federal Student Aid (FAFSA), student may be considered for additional assistance. Of all the financial aid awarded at Palm Beach Atlantic, 84 percent is not repayable, including nearly $3,000 awarded to recipients of the Academic Merit Award. Students may also be eligible for the school's Experience Scholarship or a church-related Vocation Scholarship. Interested students should call 888-GOTOPBA or go online at Palm Beach.

Four-year ROTC scholarships are available at Wheaton College through the Military Science Department. Merit scholarships based on SAT/ACT scores are also available. Wheaton has a President's Achievement Award for freshmen finalists in the National Hispanic Scholar Program and a National Achievement Scholarship for outstanding African-American students. To help with tuition and fees, Wheaton has an installment plan available for monthly or deferred payments. Illinois residents may qualify for a state scholarship worth $4,500. There is also a special grant for students interested in medical missions following graduation. Log on Wheaton or call 630-752-5005 for details. Students need to complete the FAFSA form to be considered for student aid.

Whether you are fill out an aid application for a state university or a private college, the results are the same. It is the financial figures noted on the forms that determine how much the school expect you to contribute out of pocket.

Financial Aid Glossary

- *Merit-Based Assistance* – Scholarship awards to students with a particular skill, achievement or talent
- *Need-Based Assistance* – The most common forms of need-based aid are grants, work-study programs and student loans. Students must file the *FAFSA or FAF* to be eligible.
- *Non-Need Based Aid* – Most often a student or parent loan.
- *Gift Aid* – Money that does not have to be repaid, such as grants and scholarships.
- *Self-help Aid* – Aid that requires repayment, such as student and parent loans.

HELPFUL WEB LINKS

NOTE: ALL INTERNET LINKS IN *TheCollegeTrap* ARE UNDERLINED.
TO ACTIVATE THE WEB LINKS, GO TO WWW.THECOLLEGETRAP.INFO

FREE RIDE FOR THE NATION'S BEST

The colleges are fiercely competing for highly qualified students according to an article on Foxnews.com. "Top-tier schools literally are fighting to get good students, which is good news for parents. It's a sellers market, with students doing the selling of their accomplishments and potential, and colleges offering attractive aid packages in a way of buying," according to the Fox reporter. Writing for USNews.com, Avery Comarow said, "The president of one prestigious liberal arts college likens the current climate to a bidding war between colleges determined to get the freshmen they want." Often the preparation to be part of the bidding war begins in junior high. Of the 80,000 seventh-graders to tackle the SAT® as part of Duke's Talent Identification Program, one seventh-grade student made a perfect score on the math portion of the test. In preparation for future scholarships, we strongly urge parents to encourage their young students to begin taking the SAT® as soon as possible.

PHARMACY SHORTAGE

The shortage of trained Pharmacists continues to be in the news, especially with the advancing age of the baby boomers. A pharmacy student today often receives 3 to 4 job offers before graduation as well as $80,000 to $90,000 starting salary. In some cases the student may also receive signing bonus and a willingness to repay a portion of his or her student loans. For more, click here.

AMERICA'S HOTTEST JOBS

Here's a list of the most sought-after applicants. Want to know what career is the best right now, log onto Hot Jobs.

NURSING SHORTAGE
Industry experts continue to report a shortage of qualified nurses. Registered nurses with a minimum of one-year experience may be in an enviable position. California based HRN Services places RN's and other healthcare providers in hospitals across the country with flexible hours and lucrative benefits. For more information, log onto Nursing.

START COLLEGE AS A SOPHOMORE
The surge in the number of students taking AP® tests is changing America's schools. Nearly 2 million students recently took AP exams, a whopping increase over the number of the college-level tests taken a decade ago. "The Advanced Placement Program, which began as a tiny experiment for top seniors seeking college courses and credit, has swelled to the point of altering the high school experience," notes Ben Feller at the Associated Press. "A few hundred public high schools used to offer AP; now two-thirds of them do." High scores on Advanced Placement exams can save thousands of dollars by enabling students to enter college with sophomore status. For more information, click on AP Classes.

CLEP® TESTS CAN SAVE STUDENTS THOUSANDS
The College-Level Examination Program® or CLEP®, allows students to earn college credit for what they already know. The College Board has a special web site that provides all the details at CLEP.

WISE PLANNING HELPS AVOID COLLEGE DEBT
Strategic financial planning is the main focus of the author's article published online at Urbana by Inter-Varsity Christian Fellowship.

TIPS ON CUTTING COLLEGE COSTS
High school students should read the following article on how to reduce the overall cost of attending college. Check out Crosswalk.

UNCLE SAM'S STUDENT GUIDE
Almost everything is now online including the current Student Guide.

COLLEGE MONEY
Today's military continues to be one of America's best-kept secrets when it comes to college scholarships and grants. Check out the Navy.

TALBOT'S STUDENT PLANNING BOOK
Here's a great place to get a lot of information. Log on Talbot's and click "Articles."

COLLEGE FUNDING
For an article on college finances originally published in Larry Burkett's Money Matters, click on College Funding. This is a PDF file. If the file fails to open, download Acrobat Reader, free from Adobe.

Chapter II

Choosing a College

College Admission

As a prospective college student, perhaps the one key you hold that will make a difference in your financial position when you graduate from college is the school you select. As you continue to read *TheCollegeTrap*, you'll note that we strongly encourage students to seek out a college that is seeking them. In other words, enroll where your grades and talents lead to grants and scholarships and avoid high interest student loans.

Is it worth it? Is it worth spending four or five years of your life eagerly seeking the infamous "sheep skin?" According to the latest statistics, college graduates with at least a bachelor's degree earn some $23,000 more each year than those with high school diplomas. The data shows a difference of $51,000 per year vs. $28,000. The report does not differentiate between private or state schools or between those who graduate with huge student loan debt vs. those who are debt free. You can make the difference in your favor based on the college you select.

In September and October of each year, a limited number of colleges and universities begin reviewing applications for the following fall semester. Early decision applicants may have an advantage, especially if the student would otherwise be marginal based on his or her credentials. Nearly 20-30 percent of all students apply under early decision rules. If accepted, early decision candidates must firmly commit to attending the school and immediately withdraw all other college applications.

The reason some colleges make early decisions is primarily economic. The college or university knows by mid-December how many students are securely committed for the following fall and how many openings still remain.

Whether you submit your application packet in the fall for early decision or in the spring with the remaining application pool, the school quickly scrutinizes your packet. If you did not include everything requested by the school, your application will be returned. In most cases the admissions committee reads the application as soon as it arrives. Submit your application as early as possible and well before the deadline.

If your application is complete, 2 or 3 members of the admissions committee will peruse the contents and score your application based on your overall performance. For example, a student could score a 7 or 8 on academics, a 6 or 7 on teacher and counselor recommendations, but only a 3 on extracurricular activities. Every aspect of the application is scored prior to going to the full committee for acceptance or rejection.

Some schools send recruiters to various parts of the country to meet students at their high school or one of the many college fairs. Personal contact with a college representative can prove beneficial. Those who attend a college fair are able to:

- Ask key questions of each representative,
- Collect brochures and applications,
- Get information about scholarships and financial aid.

Two-Year vs. Four-Year Degree

One of the most challenging aspects of a high school student's life is finding a college that best suits his or her needs, desires and ambitions. Some students spend years visiting colleges across the nation, while others are prone to select their parents' alma mater or a school attended by a brother or sister. Look for a college that best fits your personality, academic goals and your wallet. Your high school guidance counselor can often direct you.

In most cases, to achieve economic success in today's climate, you need a 2-year or 4-year college degree. Many companies require their new employees to hold at least a master's degree. Graduate school can be very expensive with fewer grants and scholarships available.

If you are not interested in earning a bachelor's degree or even an associate's degree, you can still pursue advanced technical study at a junior college or trade school in areas like welding, cabinet making, auto repair, or metal shop. There you can set the stage for your career leaving little student debt behind.

If you're willing to attend a local community college for your first

2 years prior to transferring to the "big name" school, the cost savings can be substantial. Rhonda Morgan, associate professor of business administration at Gordon College in Georgia, asked students to consider the cost and educational benefits of attending a 2-year school first:

"What if you could save almost half the cost of a college education? Suppose you choose to begin your college education at a 2-year community college? A student could complete the first 2 years of a 4-year degree at a fraction of the cost of a 4-year school. Studies comparing the achievement of 2-year college students with 4-year colleges and universities found that the more courses students take at the community college level, the better they do in a 4-year school.

After 2 years of study at the community college, the Bachelor's degree can then be pursued at a 4-year college or university. In the end, the Bachelor's degree comes from the 'school of choice' without the high tuition costs for all 4 years." said Professor Morgan. NOTE: Not all community college credits transfer to every college or university. Be sure to check with the 4-year institution before enrolling.

Projected Future Costs*

The following projections include the cost of tuition, room, board, books and living expenses. Add to these figures any special meal plans, unusual lab fees, additional student fees and long distance travel. The cost indicated for the 2-year public or community college reflects tuition, books and local transportation.

SCHOOL	2008/09	2009/10	2010/11	2011/12	2012/13
4-Yr Private	$38,300	$42,700	$44,600	$50,800	$54,100
4-Yr Public	$19,100	$20,600	$22,725	$24,600	$27,550
2-Yr Public	$ 3,900	$ 4,900	$ 5,850	$ 7,100	$ 7,450

*Estimated figures adjusted for inflationary factors and tuition increases.

How Many Applications?

Since 70 to 80 percent of all students file admission applications in the spring of their senior year, most high school guidance counselors recommend that students apply to as many as 5 different colleges. Two schools, for example, may be more selective in their admissions criteria and possibly a stretch or marginal for acceptance. Two others may be considered "80 percent chance" schools, while the last college is labeled a "safety school" or one where the applicant knows in advance that he or she will be accepted.

Secondary schools prepare students for the basic core curriculum courses such as English, math, and science. It is also imperative that students are prepared to compete in the most rigorous courses offered at college. Most colleges and universities look for a minimum of 16 to 18 units of college preparatory classes including:

- *English – 4 years*: including English composition, American and world literature.
- *Math – 3 to 4 years*: including geometry, algebra I and II, trigonometry, and calculus.
- *History and Geography – 2 to 3 years*: including US history, world history, US government, world cultures, civics, and geography.
- *Lab Science – 2 to 3 years*: including biology, earth science, chemistry and physics.
- *Foreign Language – 3 to 4 years:* such as French, Japanese, Russian, Spanish, German, or Latin. For those hoping to go into the Foreign Service after graduating from college, Chinese, Farsi and Arabic are critical languages of today.

In addition to the noted curriculum on the previous page, students should choose electives such as economics, computer science, art, music, communications, psychology, and drama.

Two-Year (Associate Degree)	Four-Year College (Bachelor's Degree)	Four-Plus Years (Graduate Degrees)
Surveyor	Writer	Lawyer
Air-Conditioning Tech	Teacher	Doctor
Computer Technician	Accountant	Dentist
Nurse	FBI Special Agent	Architect
Dental Hygienist	Engineer	Registered Dietitian
Medical Laboratory	Journalist	Psychologist
Commercial Artist	Insurance Agent	Minister or Priest
Restaurant Management	Investment Banker	Veterinarian
Engineering Technician	Graphic Designer	Geologist
Auto Mechanic	Public Relations	University Professor
Admin Assistant	Nutritionist	Nurse Practitioner

Well-Rounded?

What are colleges and universities looking for? One admissions director says, "You may have heard that we are looking for well-rounded students. On the contrary, we are looking for students who have excelled in a specific area, possibly a sport or talent. Combining these specialists with other classmates provides us a well-rounded student body."

Letters of Recommendation

Students should request letters of recommendation as early as possible. Provide the name of the admissions director, the school name and address and the deadline for each letter you ask someone to write. Don't simply expect letters of recommendation. Personally ask your high school guidance counselor and your teachers who are familiar with your talents, abilities, attitude and performance.

You may also wish to request letters of recommendation from your coach, your principal, or your employer if you have a part-time job, or your student pastor, all of whom are able to write about your character qualities, growth potential and drive toward success.

Advanced Placement Program®

Some of the above courses are offered as honors and advanced placement classes in both public and private high schools. The AP® classes provide students a sneak preview of college-level work in many different subjects. The classes cover extensive material at a faster pace and present stimulation for motivated students. Advanced placement classes are important for several reasons:

1) They improve the student's overall application profile. Most colleges view AP® courses as a sign of the student's willingness to accept a challenge and proof of their intellectual competence.

2) Students who pass the AP® exam at the end of each course with a score of 4 or 5 may receive college credit. This can save hundreds or even thousands of dollars in tuition fees.

3) AP® classes let a student enhance his or her grade point average by earning a grade higher then the traditional 4-point scale. An A in an AP® class scores a 5-point; a B is posted as a 4-point.

"Because colleges award different amounts of credit for each test, most students end up missing out on the tests that could result in the largest tuition savings. Tuition savvy students should take the classes and exams that result in the most savings," writes Ben Kaplan at Scholarship Coach.

Cost-Cutting Ideas

Often the biggest hurdle in selecting a college is cost. As you continue through *TheCollegeTrap,* you'll find many ways to save college costs and avoid financial bondage when you graduate.

In addition to saving money by 1) attending a community college your first 2 years, and 2) receiving college credit for passing several AP® exams, you may be able to eliminate some of the required courses through the College Level Examination Program (<u>CLEP</u>). Any one of these cost-cutting ideas could allow you to start your college career as a sophomore and save an entire year of college costs. Add lofty SAT or ACT scores and you'll have the key ingredients needed to attend college at a reduced rate.

Some students take a different approach. To give their academic appeal a boost, these students apply to schools where their national test scores, scholastic achievements, and grade point average put them well above the freshman average. Their plan is to be sought-after and receive numerous institutional scholarships.

What about tuition costs if you want to attend a college or university in another state? As the name implies, in-state tuition rates are reserved for those who are residents of that particular state. Most states will not allow you to become a state resident while you are a student. Your recourse is to work full-time in the state. Secure a driver's license and voter registration card and pay taxes through your employment. After working for one year, you can declare your residency and apply for in-state tuition at the school you wish to attend.

For a report on other ways to increase your financial aid and avoid the student loan trap, check out <u>FinAid</u> from Mark Kantowitz.

Campus Visit*

Before a campus visit, call the admissions office and schedule a tour. Visit during a regular school day to observe the normal campus bustle. If possible, arrange to sit in on a class session. Ahead of your arrival on campus, line up appointments with an admissions director, the financial aid administrator, a professor in your field of interest, and coach, if applicable. Allot enough time for everything of interest. If your visit includes an overnight stay, ask to spend the night in a campus housing facility.

Prepare for your visit by perusing the school's web site, course catalogs, and any other materials the college sent you. As you research each school, jot down questions. Become familiar with the strengths and weaknesses of each college and evaluate them further when you're on-site. Plan to bring a camera and request a map.

When you're touring a college campus, it's easy to get distracted by stately architecture, beautiful landscaping, and the pervasive energy of the campus itself. Keep in mind your family's budget and your educational goals. Here are a few things to consider on any campus visit:

- ❑ Tour the campus – including the dorms, bookstore, and library – with a guide.
- ❑ Speak to an admissions officer and attend an information session.
- ❑ Speak to the financial aid administrator.
- ❑ Observe a class in session.
- ❑ Speak to a professor in your probable major.
- ❑ Speak to a coach or athletic director (if applicable).
- ❑ Read student publications.
- ❑ Eat where the students eat.
- ❑ Interview students and ask what they like or dislike about the college.
- ❑ Explore the campus alone.

* Excerpts from www.nelliemae.com

Determining a Career Path

Today less than 25 percent of students graduate in 4 years. Studies indicate that the main reason is because students change majors as many as 3 times while in college. This increases the number of years needed to graduate and adds 20-33 percent to the total cost of the education.

One way to avoid this dilemma is to do research on various college majors from Accounting to Zoology. That alone could save a year of college spending. Interested students should log onto <u>Book of majors</u> and <u>Choosing a major</u>. For students shopping colleges based on a specialty career path, the following 2 sites will help you locate a college that meets your needs: <u>ClassesUSA</u> and <u>My Career</u>.

Ask yourself questions such as "Will I fit in?" and "Will I be challenged?" Students visiting a college in person should ask pointed questions of the administration, as well as query the students to learn what life is like on their campus.

College-bound students should make a list of the "pros" and "cons" for each college and divide them into 5 categories:

1) The distinctive nature of the school

2) The academic reputation

3) The geographical location

4) The size of the student body

5) The overall size of the campus

There are hundreds of questions you can and should ask. For example, "What type of school do I wish to attend? Do I prefer a 2-year community college, a 4-year liberal arts school, a Christian college, a technical institution, a nationally recognized state university, a small private college or a famed Ivy League school?"

Ultimately choose a college where you fit spiritually and academically. Continue to ask questions such as, "Does the school offer a major that interests me? What types of student organizations are on campus? Does the campus provide an environment for learning? Is the school ranked scholastically? Will I be challenged academically, and equally important, will my faith be challenged? What is the average SAT® and ACT® score of incoming students? Do my national test scores meet or exceed the scores of others? Is there an up-to-date resource library and research facility? Are there academic and professional organizations on campus?"

"What are my chances for acceptance? Will admittance to the college be a stretch or am I assured of enrollment? Can I apply for state residency after the first year and pay in-state tuition rates? Is the school affordable based on my budget? Is it possible to receive an institutional scholarship award? What percent of all students qualify for financial aid? Can I qualify for work-study? Will my AP® credits transfer?"

Many private and state schools offer tuition and room & board scholarships to exceptional incoming students. Some rely solely on ACT® and SAT® scores, but all are based on academic achievement. See Guaranteed Scholarships.

Other questions may include, "How easy is it to change majors and does the school offer professional counselors for every student? What is the retention rate? What is the current graduation rate? Does the college provide adequate dormitories or will I be required to live in off-campus housing? What kind of meal plan is offered in the dorms? Is the dormitory co-ed? If so, how is the gender separation handled within the dorms and bathrooms? What kind of health facility is available? Does the college or university provide up-to-date computer labs? Do most students have desktop computers or carry laptops to class? Do I need one?"

"What is the ratio of students versus faculty? What percent of all classes do professors teach versus graduate assistants? How many professors hold a Ph.D.? Are the classes small and intimate or taught in large lecture rooms? What is the average number of students per class? Do the professors have an open door policy for assisting their students? Is there a graduate program available at the school? If so, what percent of undergraduates apply for graduate school? Do the academic standards match my aspirations and allow me to achieve my designated goal after graduation? Does the school have a reputation for advancing graduates into key positions with Fortune 500 companies?"

The geographical location is often a deciding factor for many students who prefer to be near their home rather than several hours away by air. If the school is out of state, you may ask, "Is the cost of transportation included in the budget? Is the community slow-paced or primarily academically focused? Finally, how safe is the campus? What are the crime statistics for the campus and surrounding area?" Some students prefer a large school while others want to know everyone on campus and enjoy a feeling of camaraderie. More questions might be: "How large is the student body? What is the ratio of male to female students? Do most students return home on weekends? Is the campus a walking campus, a bicycle campus, or do I need an automobile? Are automobile expenses figured into my overall budget? Are there sororities and fraternities on campus? If so, what percent of the student population are members and would I need to become a member to fit in? What do the students do for fun? What percent of the student body is involved in intramural and varsity sports?"

Community Service

Community service is very important to most admission directors. Those who spend weeks or months serving on mission trips in a foreign country are often praised and encouraged. Current research however, indicates that many schools look more favorably upon students who have participated in national organizations such as Habitat for Humanity and Special Olympics.

Rhodes College in Memphis, Tennessee provides a 4-year scholarship for students who have demonstrated a high level of commitment to community service. Winners of The Bonner Scholars Program make a commitment of ten hours per week to service projects and service-learning activities and select summer service projects, jobs or internships around the world. Award includes a stipend of $3,500 per year.

Application Essay

(An essay is) "...without question, the most difficult and the most important element over which you have control in the admissions process. A well-written essay will differentiate the truly exciting student from the merely good one, and tip the scale in favor of the former," noted G. Gary Ripple, Ph.D., and Director of Admissions at Lafayette College in Easton, Pennsylvania.

Not every college requires an application essay. Those that do require it place a considerable amount of importance on the writing.

The following article on essay preparation by John C. Conkright, Dean of Admissions, Randolph-Macon College, Ashland, Virginia is used with permission of the author:

"If you are like most students, you see the college essay as just another hurdle you must jump on the way to being accepted at the college of your choice. In fact, the essay is a rare opportunity to "talk" directly to the college's admissions committee and help them see you as thinking and feeling person, rather than simply a set of impersonal statistics.

Except for the interview, it is your only chance to share your thoughts, insights, and opinions and highlight your maturity and outlook on life. If you see the college essay as an opportunity -- then it is clearly worth the extra effort and time put forth in writing it.

The college essay is extremely important for 2 major reasons: First of all, it enables the college admissions office to personally evaluate your communications skills and your ability to convey your thoughts. Secondly, it enables them to learn more about you as a person. A well-written essay can speak worlds about your attitudes, feelings, personal qualities, imagination and creativity.

Many schools will either give you a topic to write about or present several specific topics from which you must choose. Others may simply suggest general topics or give you total freedom to write about something that interests or concerns you. Here are a few hints about your topic:

- Narrow your topic; be as specific as possible.
- The easiest topic to write about is you. If you choose to write about yourself, remember that little incidents and facts are often the most revealing concerning character and outlook.
- Do not be afraid to write about something that you think is a little different. A unique topic or approach is often refreshing to a college admissions officer.

Before sitting down to write your essay, spend some time organizing your thoughts. Develop a framework for your essay so it will have a logical progression from one idea to the next Consider your purpose in writing, what you want to convey, and the tone that you think is most appropriate for the topic. Decide on a style that is comfortable for you, not one that you think the college admissions committee prefers.

Remember, you do not have to get it right the first time! Write the first draft with the main focus on content. Then set it aside for a day or 2 and reread it with a fresh perspective making necessary changes including organization, style, grammar and spelling.

Once you have rewritten your first draft, you may wish to try it out on your family, friends and English teacher or guidance counselor.

While the final product and final "voice" should be yours, they may be able to offer helpful suggestions for improvement.

Your college essay, along with your high school record, standardized test scores and extracurricular involvement will provide the basis upon which the college makes its admissions decision. A well-written essay can affect that final decision in a very positive way. Keep this in mind and take full advantage of the opportunity the college essay affords you."

Some "dos" and "don'ts:"

- Do think "small" and write about something you know well.
- Do reveal yourself in your writing.
- Do show rather than tell.
- Do write in your own "voice" and style.
- Don't write what you think others want to read.
- Don't exaggerate or write to impress.
- Don't use a flowery, inflated or pretentious style.
- Don't neglect the technical part of your essay (grammar, spelling and sentence structure.)
- Don't ramble -- say what you have to say and conclude.

Class Rank vs. National Tests

For years, scholars have written volumes of books outlining what is the most important aspect in the college admissions process. Many have retained the traditional view that grade point average and class rank are the deciding factors. Still others tout the power and prestige of the national test scores. Most agree it is the combination of high school courses, grade point average, class ranking, extracurricular activities and the essays that help determine the applicant's preparedness for college.

Referring to the attention given the national testing program, Dr. Gary Ripple adds, "There is such a great variation among high schools in the quality of teaching, the quality of courses offered, the quality of textbooks and the consistency of grading policies, that admission committees perceive SAT®/ACT® scores as a common denominator. While standardized test scores are not as important as the high school transcript, they serve as a convenient screening device for admission committees faced with thousands of applications…"

The new SAT® is comprised of 3 sections including reading comprehension and sentence completion; math, which is consistent with the current testing of basic arithmetic, algebra I, and geometry, and some algebra II; writing, devoted to grammar, usage; and a timed essay requiring students to take a position on an issue.

Each section in the SAT® is scored on a 200-800 scale, with a maximum combined score of 2400. Even Wall Street firms are looking at SAT® scores. "More and more companies are looking for ways to sort through thousands of candidates," said John Challenger, CEO of Challenger Gray & Christmas, "The SAT® score is a simple way of cutting down the pile."

Because of the increased competition for institutional scholarships and admission into the best colleges and universities, students should receive tutorial assistance prior to their final national test date, regardless of whether they attended a Christian school, private academy, a public high school or were schooled at home.

The Princeton Review offers courses in major cities to help students be more competitive in their PSAT®, SAT®, SAT II® or ACT® scores. In addition, they publish the average test scores for incoming students at hundreds of colleges and universities across the country. Interested students may contact them on the Web at Review or by calling 800-2REVIEW. Internet active students can also check out the Kaplan Educational Center for books on testing preparation at Kaptest.

OUTSTANDING OPPORTUNITIES

NOTE: ALL INTERNET LINKS IN *TheCollegeTrap* ARE UNDERLINED.
TO ACTIVATE THE WEB LINKS, GO TO WWW.THECOLLEGETRAP.INFO

ESSAY PREP NOW MORE CRITICAL FOR NEW SAT®

The online College Journal from the Wall Street Journal offers a course on essay writing at EssayEdge. Since a timed essay plays a major role in scoring the SAT® exam, students need to be prepared for writing an essay under pressure as part of the national testing program.

SAT® TEST PREP ONLINE

Need help preparing for the national tests? A high school senior in the Atlanta area scored a perfect score on her SAT® test last year and attributed much of her success to practice exams. Check out the Princeton Review web site at Practice Test and take a demo exam of the newest version. Writing for Fox News, David S. Hirschman reports that students are stressing out and looking for ways to boost their scores. "The changes to the test have caused a lot of confusion and consternation," said Jennifer Karan, national director of SAT® and ACT® programs for the Kaplan test preparation company. "The result has been a large jump in the number of students taking practice tests and enrolling in courses and private tutoring," Karan also reported that in the last year the number of students taking Kaplan's free practice test has jumped 78 percent. Log on Kaplan.

ACT TEST PREP ONLINE

Log onto ACT at a glance for important details about the American College Test, along with a free ACT prep test. There's also an ACT® prep course available at Prep Course, and a study guide at Test Prep.

MATH PREP ONLINE
One of the key factors in qualifying for a scholarship rests on the student's math scores. A Georgia company is promoting a fee-based online math program available 24/7. Check out iCoachMath for additional information.

LOVE A GAME BOY? LOOK AT THIS
The Princeton Review put together a Pocket Prep for the new SAT that's smaller than a Game Boy. It's basically a handheld interactive Tutor from Franklin Electronic Publishers to help you improve your national test scores no matter where you are. Check it out at SAT-2400.

COLLEGE SEARCH
The Princeton Review has multiple links to help you research different colleges plus ways to increase your national test scores. For details on this and other college search sites, log on Princeton Review, or Campus Tours.

HOMESCHOOLERS AT CEDARVILLE
Located just north of Dayton, Ohio; Cedarville University is a member of the Council for Christian Colleges & Universities. Many of the 2,800 students from around the world are former homeschoolers in such fields as engineering, broadcasting, Bible, music, communications, nursing, criminal justice, and multimedia technology. The University also offers both Air Force and Army ROTC scholarships for those who qualify. To learn more, call 1-800-CEDARVILLE. For a complete list of CCCU member schools, see Christian Colleges.

FULL SCHOLARSHIP BIBLE COLLEGE
A liberal arts Christian college in Moberly, Missouri offers every full time student a scholarship to cover tuition. Like all post-secondary schools, students must pay for student fees and room and board. Federal student aid is available including Pell Grants for those who qualify. For more information, click on Central Christian.

BLACK COLLEGES & UNIVERSITIES
Called the best kept secret in higher education on their website, EducationUSA profiles 117 historically black schools across the nation. For more information, log onto BACU.

VETERAN'S BENEFITS HIGHLIGHTED
For the brave men and women who have just left the service and are looking for educational benefits, log onto Veterans for scholarship updates. (This is a non-government site.)

Chapter III

What about Homeschoolers?

Obsolete Education?

Are the government schools in America obsolete? "Yes," according to Microsoft's Bill Gates, writes Michael Smith, president of <u>Homeschool Legal Defense Association</u>. Addressing the National Education Summit on High Schools, Gates said, "Even when our high schools are working exactly as designed, they cannot teach our kids what they need to know today."

Higher education institutions often speak about wanting a wide diversity of students on their campuses. Students educated at home certainly add to that diversity. The colleges use the same criteria in evaluating students including grade point average, admissions interview, application essays, SAT® and ACT® test scores, and recommendations.

Those schooled at home may have an edge over other students. "A student with only a paper trail of academics risks being lost in the crowd and does not necessarily come out on top when competing for slots at selective colleges," writes Cafi Cohen, author of *And What About College.*

Homeschool families may have an advantage in the application process as well. "Just as they have customized homeschooling to fit their educational philosophy and their student's interests and goals, families can tailor application documentation to focus on the student's strengths," notes Cohen.

Parents of homeschoolers must be prime record keepers, documenting every scholastic achievement and accomplishment. "Some colleges and universities consider themselves highly innovative and continually look for students with non-traditional backgrounds and non-traditional documentation. A high quality portfolio may well impress admissions officers at those schools," added Cohen.

Students with a completed homeschool transcript and significant national test scores may be accepted at America's best colleges and universities. Parents should not restrict themselves to government high school requirements, but rather look for ways to exceed those requirements in areas where the student is especially talented. This helps to demonstrate to the admissions committee that the student far exceeds common high school standards.

Student Transcript

"A transcript is crucial for homeschooled high school graduates," writes Inge Cannon, Executive Director of Education Plus at edplus. com. "The transcript summarizes and reports in a concise way the total educational profile of the student's experience. Behind that transcript should stand a portfolio of work samples, bibliography of resources used, detailed test information, anecdotal records, recommendations from employers and directors of extracurricular activities," says Cannon.

"If you know your graduate is college-bound, check with the admissions officers of the schools of choice to identify their requirements or guidelines," she adds.

In some states, homeschool graduates are required to successfully pass a GED test. Inge Cannon is adamantly opposed to the GED. "A diploma by way of the GED tends to carry a negative stigma," says Cannon. "The homeschooling parent has to accept the responsibility for issuing a diploma and ultimately certifying the student's status as a graduate. I believe the tutorial advantage of home education does so much more for a student that it is sad to see parents sell their young people short by granting a GED equivalency diploma."

Cannon notes that it takes only 15 college credits to validate a homeschool diploma. Students can complete 15 credit hours online at one of the many colleges offering classes over the Internet.

"Homeschooling is a calling. It is rewarding, but it's also hard," writes Zan Tyler, Media Consultant for Broadman and Holman Publishers, and homeschool editor for Christian Resources at LifeWay. com. A noted author, Tyler says that the hardest part is the daily pressure and concern regarding the student's welfare. "I know their lives are in God's hands, yet questions like, 'Am I giving them everything they need? Are we covering enough material in school? How are they doing spiritually?' seem never-ending.'"

For guidance in this area, see *7 Tools for Cultivating Your Child's*

Potential, by Zan Tyler at <u>Online Bookstore</u>, an excellent addition to your homeschool library.

After 21 years of homeschooling 3 students, Tyler says her homeschool career has officially ended. "But I am finding that my passion for homeschooling is growing, not waning," said Tyler.

"In the homeschooling environment, we have the freedom to constantly evaluate our children academically, socially, spiritually, and morally. If we don't like what we see, we can intervene and make adjustments. Homeschool is a process, and that process consists of constantly fine-tuning the program. The ability to tailor-make a curriculum – a program of instruction – for our children is one of the most compelling reasons to homeschool, and yet this process of choosing curriculum is one of the most intimidating tasks parents face," added Tyler.

"After years of homeschooling, and thousands of dollars spent, and hundreds of mistakes made, the following is my advice on what to remember during your homeschool journey:

1) There is no such thing as the perfect curriculum.

2) Choosing curriculum is a fluid process and not an exact science.

3) Some things will be perfect for one child but not for another.

4) You will make some great choices that will work well for you and your family.

5) Don't be a slave to your curriculum. You can adapt and enhance any curriculum by employing your own ingenuity and creativity, coupled with your knowledge of how your child learns and responds. Above all, curriculum is not an end in itself – it is a means to an end."

(Ed. Note: Tyler is one of America's homeschool pioneers. By holding her 2 sons out of the public school system, the State

Superintendent of Education in South Carolina threatened to put her in jail. Tyler ignored the threat and went on to homeschool her 2 sons and a daughter through high school. All have since gone on to college with multiple athletic and academic scholarships.)

Brian Ray, Ph.D., author of the *Worldwide Guide to Homeschooling*, and President of the National Home Education Research Institute at nheri. org, notes:

"If a veteran homeschooler says there is one best way and one best curriculum for all homeschoolers, you should quickly depart from their presence."

"I hope I have made it clear in my book that there is no one best way for all homeschoolers to follow. Homeschooling lets parents carefully and wisely evaluate curriculum materials and instructional approaches. In choosing materials and strategies, parents should consider their own educational philosophy and talents, their child's special gifts and unique needs, as well as their family's unique character. In the United States, parents spend, on average, $300 to $600 per year per child for home education materials."

When asked if all curriculum materials are religious based, Ray acknowledged, "At this historical moment, most homeschoolers are Christian However, not all are. Many textbooks, science kits, and other materials appear religiously neutral. Curriculum producers have developed so many products that almost anyone of any religious persuasion can find plenty of materials to purchase or use."

According to *The Campus Life Guide to Christian Colleges and Universities*, Christian colleges are more likely to agree with the philosophical reasons for homeschooling, and many are actively recruiting students schooled at home. See Patrick Henry College.

Well-known homeschool advocate and author, Cathy Duffy, has

written a book entitled, *100 Top Picks for Homeschool Curriculum.* Published by Broadman & Holman Publishers, 100 Top Picks is an excellent starting point for those seeking advice on curriculum. Read more about the veteran homeschooler at Duffy Reviews.

Some states are slow in recognizing and accepting homeschoolers on a par with other high school graduates. Once the college admissions committee accepts the student, the process of applying for financial aid is the same as with any other student.

Students who have been homeschooled are asked to complete the same FAFSA or Financial Aid Profile® forms. Based on the information provided, the need analysis methodology is used to determine financial need. Like students who attended public or private high schools, the colleges will evaluate the student's national test scores to help determine admissions acceptance and scholarships.

Armed with solid performance figures and transcripts, homeschoolers may qualify for more college grants and scholarship than their counterpart from the government schools.

Chapter IV

Scholarships & Grants

When to Start

It's never too late to begin looking for scholarships, nor is it ever too early! Ben Kaplan, who affectionately calls himself the Scholarship Coach, suggests, "There is a sizeable array of scholarships that students as young as sixth grade can apply for today. Applying for scholarships is partially a numbers game. A variety of factors beyond your control can affect the outcome of any given scholarship program or contest. Only by applying for a large number of scholarships can you minimize such factors."

We recommend you first look in your own city or state before engaging in national competition. Many organizations such as the Elks Club, Kiwanis, Jaycees, Lions Club, American Legion, YMCA, 4-H and the Chamber of Commerce provide scholarships to local members or family members.

Scholarships Myths

Every year thousands of people believe the bogus story related to all the lost or unused scholarships. Many are lured into spending hundreds of dollars with scholarship search firms that promise to do all the required paperwork to search for those missing dollars. These firms even guarantee a minimum of $1,000 in financial aid "or your money back." Don't get caught believing that myth! *Scholarships rarely go unused.*

The government provides the bulk of all funding via student loans, federal grants, work-study and V.A benefits. Nearly 20 percent of all financial aid is provided by the colleges. State grants equal some 15 to 17 percent of all student aid. The private scholarship pool, on the other hand, is extremely small. Only about 1 percent of all scholarships offered are from private donors.

According to the College Board, some 300,000 people are cheated every year by scholarship scams despite efforts by the Federal Trade Commission to shut down the scam artists. To be sure, locate the city and state for any scholarship search firm you are considering. Then check with the Better Business Bureau to see if the firm has multiple complaints charged against them.

The Federal Trade Commission (FTC) notes that families may also fall prey to verbal claims such as:
- "You can't get this information anywhere else"
- "I just need your credit card or bank account number to hold

the scholarship"
- "You have been selected by a national foundation to receive a scholarship"
- "You're a finalist in a scholarship contest"
- "The money has already been reserved for you"
- "Listen to what others are saying about us"

Another myth often held by students is that the competition is too stiff. Charlotte Thomas, Career and Education Editor for Peterson's, points out that scholarship contests are not just for valedictorians but are open to every student. She also notes that the number one myth heard every year concerns the "billions" of scholarship dollars that go unclaimed, a claim frequently immortalized by the media.

Company Paid Tuition

This is one of the most over-stated examples of unused scholarship money. The Company Tuition Plan is not available to every student. In fact, only those who work for an employer willing to pay for them to return to school full-time or part-time are eligible. These are private funds and should not be mistaken as unused student financial aid dollars.

Those who are eligible may be reimbursed up to $5,250 for tuition, books and travel. The fees paid by the employer are taxable. All other expenses may be deducted on Schedule A, Form 1040, when filing federal income taxes. Internal Revenue Service rules change frequently and participants in this plan should consult their company personnel office for changes.

Dos and Don'ts

No matter what scholarship you apply for, there are a few dos and don'ts you need to know. First, always apply on time. You may want to keep a file on each scholarship with the address, the application deadline and the progress on each item. When possible, submit your application 2 to 3 weeks before the deadline. Some students wait until the last minute, rushing through their application and essay, and end up making a very poor impression on the scholarship review committee.

Some applications require a long explanation of why you should receive the scholarship award. Put your answer down in a clear and thought-provoking manner. Those who read all the applications look for expressed ambitions and want to know what makes you different from every other applicant.

Many scholarship applications as well as admissions applications require an essay. Some people consider the essay the most important part of the application.

Some students send out as many as 20 to 30 applications. Learn who is sponsoring each scholarship and look up each sponsor on the Internet or in a library. Customize your essay to fit *the sponsor's* interests. The more you know about the organization, the better your chances of winning the award.

Don't brag about yourself and list your credentials. Emphasize your achievements and leadership skills. Be who you are and present your essay in a logical, well-planned manner. Throw away your Thesaurus and buy a copy of *The Elements of Style* by William Strunk and E.B. White.

The key is to write something original, something about you that will compel the reader to continue reading your essay. Both scholarship committees and admissions committees want to understand what motivates you. You may want to write about your extracurricular activities or volunteer work. Share how a particular experience affected you and what you learned from the experience. One admissions director said he would rather read why a particular book was important to you than to hear about the book itself. He then went on to say he would rather read about a conversation you had with someone on a trip than to read the details of the trip.

Don't forget the 5 W's: Who, What, Why, When, and Where. Once you have all 5 W's covered, you may be able to stop writing but be sure your essay and the entire application is neat. Ask your parents or a teacher to proofread it. Just in case you make a mistake, you may want to photocopy the application and fill out a few draft copies before completing the official form.

If you need letters from your teachers, pastor or coaches, be sure to give them plenty of time. Ask them not to write a "To Whom it May Concern" letter. Provide them with the correct names and addresses. Your entire application packet should be as personal as possible.

Some merit-based scholarships may ask for copies of your high school transcript, your class ranking, and your national test scores. Send a short cover letter thanking the organization for considering you for their scholarship award.

In most cases, to earn a top-flight scholarship, you must have exceptional grades and national test scores. To improve your national test scores, check out the following at Practice Test.

Financial Aid Packages

When the colleges put together their financial aid packages, each one is unique. There is fierce competition for top awards. A student with a strong grade point average and a record of community service who scored high on the national tests and passed several AP classes or took joint-enrollment college classes may receive a large merit scholarship.

On the other hand, a student whose scores are average may receive financial aid offers primarily made up of high cost student loans. The difference between the cost of attendance and the aid offered in the financial aid package is the amount you and your parents are expected to contribute.

One word of caution: If you receive an outside scholarship, it's possible that the amount of aid offered from the college or university could be reduced by the same amount. If, however, the college does not meet your full need, then an outside scholarship can be used to reduce your personal contribution.

Since the colleges and universities are reluctant to offer straight discounts to incoming students struggling with sticker shock, many schools will offset the high costs and remain competitive by providing grant-aid.

One student received a "leadership scholarship" after the college learned that the family could not afford the tuition at a private Christian school. The scholarship was not a published award but rather offered as part of an overall recruitment effort. No matter how the funds are distributed or what they are called, a discount or scholarship, the award still serves to minimize student debt. Sometimes colleges use grants as a recruiting tool and grant money on the basis of merit instead of need. As a result, academic scholarships are frequently saved as an admission bonus for those students with elevated SAT® and ACT® scores, regardless of where they have been schooled. See Guaranteed Scholarships.

Nationally, every college and university will base their institutional scholarship awards on the student's demonstrated need and scholastic achievement. Then too, incoming students may find that negotiations can land a tuition reduction based on how the school perceives the student at the time of application.

Negotiations may become an ongoing way of life for all students in the future. One national university invites students to notify them if another college offers a better financial aid package. In some cases, the university will match the other award or even upgrade it.

Admission officers and financial aid staff do not use the term "negotiate." Even though many negotiate on a regular basis, most will not admit it nor use the term in their discussions with you.

High school students in their sophomore and junior year should take the Preliminary Scholastic Assessment Test (PSAT®). Those who score high on the PSAT® may win one of the 7,000 prestigious National Merit Scholarships. Other participants may earn recognition as a National Merit Semifinalist which also looks good on a college application. Check out Merit Scholarship, or write the National Merit Scholarship Corporation, 1560 Sherman Avenue, Evanston, Illinois 60201.

National Testing

Many scholarships are awarded based on the Scholastic Assessment Test® or the American College Testing Assessment®. The 2 tests are entirely different. Some educators believe that the SAT® is more of an aptitude test to evaluate a student's ability to do college-level work while the ACT® is more of an achievement test, evaluating the skills already mastered. A student may take both tests each year beginning in the seventh grade to help parents and teachers assess the student's overall progress.

Schools are fiercely competing for highly qualified students. Writing for *USNews.com*, Avery Comarow said, "The president of one prestigious liberal arts college likens the current climate to a bidding war between colleges determined to get the freshmen they want."

Often the preparation to be part of the bidding war begins in junior high. Of the 80,000 seventh-graders to tackle the SAT® as part of Duke's Talent Identification Program, one seventh-grade student made a perfect score on the math portion of the test. In preparation for future scholarships, we strongly urge parents to encourage their young students to begin taking the SAT® as soon as possible.

When you take the SAT® or ACT®, you are not competing with students in your class, or in your junior high or high school, or even in your state. You will be competing globally against students in Europe, Asia and the Far East who take the SAT® and ACT®, along with the Test of English as a Foreign Language (TOELF®) before being accepted into an American college. Be aware also of the competition from those in the Northeast and on the West coast of the United Sates where many students begin taking the SAT® in the 7th and 8th grades, often followed by multiple preparation classes

Here's the key that opens the scholarship door. Prepare ahead by receiving concentrated exam preparation from qualified tutors for both tests. There is an overwhelming acceptance of the national testing programs for academic scholarships and admission into the best schools.

Students seeking merit-based awards should consider tutorial assistance prior to their final testing date, whether schooled at home or in a public or private high school. We cannot emphasize this enough.

The Princeton Review offers courses to help students become more competitive as they maximize their PSAT®, SAT®, SAT II® or ACT® scores. This nationally recognized organization assists students in overall preparation. Student scores often advance well over 100 points between their junior and senior testing dates. The Princeton Review also publishes the average test scores for incoming students at hundreds of colleges and universities across the country for comparative purposes. You can find them by clicking Review, or calling 800-2REVIEW.

You can also check out the Kaplan Educational Center for new books on standardized testing preparation. The firm maintains links to information on nursing, law school, medicine, accounting and other tutorial aids, plus tips on budgeting, saving money while at college, and avoiding problems with credit cards. The College Board also maintains a web site at Collegeboard for the Scholastic Assessment Test preparation materials.

Robert C. Byrd Scholarship

Students who are eligible for the Robert C. Byrd scholarship receive $1,500 each year for 4 years. The financial award may be used at any college or university in the United States. Students must apply before high school graduation. The scholarship is named after the former Senate Majority Leader, Robert Byrd. The program is federally funded and administered by state officials. Unlike the Pell Grant and the Supplemental Educational Opportunity Grant, the Byrd Scholarship is not based on financial need. The total number of scholarships available is determined by federal appropriations per Congressional district. *(See Appendix Four)*

Corporate Scholarships

Many scholarships are sponsored by America's most respected entrepreneurs. Atlanta-based Chick-fil-A Corporation awards hundreds of $1,000 Leadership Scholarships every year to their brightest employees. The top 25 recipients also receive the S. Truett Cathy Award of $1,000. Chick-fil-A is a partner with Berry College in Rome, Georgia, providing a $24,000 WinShape scholarship every year to one new student. For more information on the WinShape award, call 800-448-6955.

The Eight & Forty Nursing Scholarship is sponsored by the American Legion specifically for Registered Nurses seeking a Bachelor's or Master's degree in the lung and respiratory field. The organization provides 22 scholarships annually worth $25,000. To learn more about this and other scholarships, log onto American and highlight scholarship information, or send $3.95 to American Legion Headquarters, P.O. Box 1050, Indianapolis, Indiana 46206 and request the current edition of *Need a Lift*.

The National Science Teachers sponsors a competitive award called ExploraVision that encourages K-12 students of all interest, skill and ability levels to create and explore a vision of future technology by combining their imaginations with the tools of science. For more information, call or write NSTA, 1840 Wilson Blvd., Arlington, Virginia 22201, 888-255-4242 Awards.

The Coca-Cola Scholars Program is open to all high school seniors in the United States. Every year, 50 students are recognized as National Scholars and each receives a $20,000 award for college. An additional 200 Regional Scholars receive a $4,000 award. The Coca-Cola Foundation also provides a Hispanic Scholarship Fund and a "First to Go" scholarship designed for students who are the first in their family to attend college.

The Siemens Westinghouse Science and Technology Competition is a national program for independent research completed in high school. The top prize is $120,000. There are also 6 individual regional winners of $20,000 each ($30,000 if divided among 2 or 3 team members). The program is designed to promote and encourage students to undertake individual or team research projects in science, math and technology. The project may also include submissions in math and the biological and physical sciences. Specific information is found at <u>Siemens</u>.

The National Academy of American Scholars (NAAS) sponsors the Easley National Scholarships for high school seniors. Applicants must be high school seniors, US residents, and have been accepted into an accredited 4-year academic program in order to qualify.

The NAAS also sponsors the National NAAS-II Scholarship for college freshmen. Applicants must be US citizens and currently enrolled in an accredited college or university. Scholarships range from 4-year renewable awards of $10,000, $6,000 and $4,000 to smaller scholarships and cash awards. Interested students may log on <u>NAAS</u> for details.

The National Foundation for the Elks annually awards 4-year scholarships to 500 of the top students in the nation. The "Most Valuable Student" awards range from $1,000 per year to $7,500 per year for the 4-year period. Applicants must be in the top 5 percent of their class, have leadership qualities and indicate financial need. Students are not required to be a member or related to a member, but must be recommended by a local Elks Club.

National Security Agency

The National Security Agency Scholarship Program may be one of Uncle Sam's best-kept secrets. The NSA offers an outstanding opportunity to students studying math, computer science, computer engineering, electrical engineering or foreign languages. To be considered for the prestigious award, high school students must apply for the NSA-Stokes Scholarship Program at the beginning of their senior year. NSA staff members carefully screen every application and only 15 to 20 new candidates are selected annually. Those accepted receive 4 years of tuition, books and fees at the school of their choice, a salary of $20,000 to $25,000, a guarantee of employment after graduation, plus housing allowance and travel costs to and from Fort Meade, Maryland, each summer.

What's the catch? NSA scholarship participants must maintain a 3-point grade point average while in college and agree to work for the Agency near Washington, DC during the summer months and for 4 and one half years after graduation. Those who fail to complete their assignment are required to reimburse the government for tuition and books.

Prerequisites for the NSA-Stokes Scholarship Program are similar to those required for acceptance into America's military academies. Key areas include a strong national test score (minimum 1600 SAT and 25 ACT), a solid high school transcript (a grade point average of 3-point or higher), outstanding references, community service, strong work ethic, and leadership ability. Beginning compensation after graduation is highly competitive with outside corporate wages.

For more information and an application, write the National Security Agency, Attn: Stokes, 9800 Savage Road, Suite 6779, Fort Meade, Maryland 20755-6840 or call 410-854-4725. For details online, see NSA and follow this procedure: Once the website opens, click on "Stokes Educational Scholarship Program" found in the box on the right side of the webpage.

Athletic Scholarships

Students wanting to play college athletics should begin planning in their high school freshman year. For professional suggestions concerning a timeline and how to put together an athletic resume, students can go online to: Recruit Me, or Scholarship Timeline.

Reference guides for nearly every sport may be purchased directly from the publisher. Take a look at The Sport Source or call 800-862-3092.

Athletes looking for playing experience at the college level should select the school that best fits their athletic and academic abilities, as well as their financial budget. There are specialized sports organizations that help student-athletes find the right school, the right coach, and the right academic fit.

Recruiting Teams

There are several national recruiting organizations for college-bound student-athletes. Some of the noted organizations include the Interactive Sports Profile, Scouting Network, College Sports Scholarships, and Athletic Scholarships.

Athletic Associations

Different athletic associations sanction all sports activities and determine how much and how many scholarships schools can award. Every year approximately 150 athletes receive a $5,000 award from the NCAA to attend graduate school.

For student-athletes to be eligible to play, they must first register and be certified by Association's Initial-Eligibility Clearinghouse including the National Collegiate Athletic Association, (NCAA), and the National Association of Intercollegiate Athletics (NAIA).

Most often the largest amount of scholarship money goes to the college basketball and football athletes. Colleges and universities use scholarships to recruit the best players.

The NAIA is strong among smaller colleges and universities. A student attending one of these schools could qualify for a scholarship in soccer, field hockey, lacrosse, cross country or rowing. There are thousands of scholarship opportunities available today for the top athletes, regardless of the sport.

Finally, there are specific rules that govern students and coaches when recruited to play a particular sport for a college or university. Check out Student Eligibility for a review of the rules under Division I recruiting, and be wary of coaches and recruiters offering extra benefits or money before or after enrolling in their school.

Title IX

There are many college sports where men and women can qualify for scholarships. The NCAA watches over 22 different sports. The Title IX decision governing college athletics was well received by some athletes. Yet, others were clearly hurt by the landmark decision as their particular sport was eliminated in order to budget for women's athletics.

Title IX mandates that colleges provide equal financial budgets for both men's and women's sports. The highly charged decision was first rendered in 1972, but it was not until the mid-1990's that the government began enforcing the rule. To learn the history behind the decision and the current status, log on Title IX.

Student Grants

The Federal Pell Grant is an entitlement grant based on a student's established need, citizenship and enrollment in an undergraduate course of study. Since the grant is directly linked to the Expected Family Contribution (EFC), it does not take into consideration personal debt, high medical expenses or private school tuition payments. You or your family could be inundated with debt and still not qualify for a Pell Grant.

The Pell is one of the government's biggest programs, and also one of the most changeable. The grant is available to undergraduate students or those taking post baccalaureate courses required for teacher certification.

The EFC is based on both income and assets. There is a cutoff whereby students may have an EFC too high to qualify for a Pell Grant, usually somewhere in the $3,000 range. Families with an EFC above $3,000 could still qualify for the Pell based on the number of members in the family or the number of family members in college.

If you're accepted at a college or university that allows federal assistance, you need to file a Free Application for Federal Student Aid (FAFSA), regardless of income and assets. It's possible to be turned down one year and qualify for a Pell Grant the following year. Both the Pell Gant and the SEOG (below) are administered through the college financial aid office.

Federal Supplemental Grant

If your family's income is reduced because of unusual circumstances, i.e., job loss, divorce or major illness, you may qualify for a Supplemental Educational Opportunity Grant (SEOG) in addition to the Pell. As with the Pell Grant, the SEOG is campus-based. The government provides the money directly to the colleges, who then distribute up to $4,000 per year to those with the greatest need.

State Grants

Many state governments provide special grants for students attending a state college. In some cases, the grant money is labeled a 'tuition equalization grant' and is available to offset higher tuition costs at private schools as well. Some states allow students to attend a college or university across the country and still receive a grant award.   *(See Appendix Three)*

In other cases, the funds may be tied directly to the state's talent needs. If a state is in need of nurses, medical technicians, math or science teachers, they may allow an undergraduate student to borrow from the state grant funds. Providing the student is employed in the state for one or more years following graduation, the funds are not repayable. If the student leaves the state or the field of study, the funds are then considered a loan and repayable with interest.

Federal Work-Study Program

Although not a true grant, the work-study program is campus-based and has several advantages. Students employed through the program normally work on campus requiring little or no transportation time or expense. They may earn as much as $2,000 to $3,000 in a school year. The program is administered through the financial aid department and the money earned is neither taxed nor counted as income when applying for financial aid the following year.

The work-study jobs at most colleges are highly diversified. A student may assist a science professor doing research, or work in the admissions office doing clerical work and greeting in-coming high school students. The college library or even the alumni office may provide interesting work. One student worked as a life guard while overseeing the university's swimming team during their morning workouts.

The Federal Work-Study program, or any combination of work-study programs, offers valuable experience in a local work setting. It can be a valuable ally in a complete funding plan for college, especially when coupled with grants or scholarships.

Federal Loan that Becomes a Grant

A student loan should always be considered the "last resort." The Federal Perkins Loan may be an exception. One hundred percent of the loan is service-cancelable under the following conditions:

TEACHING: 1) A full time teacher in a public or other nonprofit elementary or secondary school with a high concentration of students from low income families; 2) A full time special education teacher in a public or other nonprofit elementary or secondary school system; 3) A full time teacher, in a public or other nonprofit elementary or secondary school system, who teaches mathematics, science, foreign languages, bilingual education, or any other field of expertise where the state agency determines a shortage, or in a school system serving low-income students. For a complete listing of all teacher shortage areas within the US, log onto Teachers. (See cancellation rate below.)

EARLY INTERVENTION SERVICES: A full time qualified professional provider of early intervention to infants and toddlers with disabilities. (See cancellation rate below.)

LAW ENFORCEMENT OR CORRECTIONS OFFICER: A full time law enforcement officer or corrections officer for a local, State or Federal law enforcement or corrections agency. (See cancellation rate below.)

NURSE OR MEDICAL TECHNICIAN: A full time nurse or a full time medical technician providing health care services. Details on the forgiveness program are found online at Perkins. (See cancellation rate below.)

CHILD OR FAMILY SERVICE AGENCY: A full time employee of an eligible public or private nonprofit child or family service agency who is providing or supervising the provision of services to high-risk children from low-income communities and the families.

CANCELLATION RATE FOR ALL THE ABOVE: For each year of service, 15 percent of the original principal loan and interest for the first and second years; 20 percent of the original principal loan and interest for the third and fourth years; and 30 percent of the original principal loan amount for the fifth year.

HEAD START: A full time staff member in the educational component of a Head Start program operated for a period comparable to a full school year.

CANCELLATION RATE: For each completed year of service: 15 percent of the original principal loan amount.

MILITARY: Up to 50 percent of the principal amount of loan canceled as a member of the Armed Forces in an area of hostilities.

CANCELLATION RATE: For each year served, 12 ½ percent of the original loan.

VOLUNTEER SERVICE: Up to 70 percent of the original principal amount as 1) a volunteer under the Peace Corps Act; 2) a volunteer under the Domestic Volunteer Service Act of 1973.

CANCELLATION RATE: 15 percent of the original principal loan amount for each of the first and second 12-month periods of service; 20 percent of the original principal loan amount for each of the third and fourth 12-month periods of service.

SCHOLARSHIP OPPORTUNITIES

NOTE: ALL INTERNET LINKS IN *TheCollegeTrap* ARE UNDERLINED.
TO ACTIVATE THE WEB LINKS, GO TO WWW.THECOLLEGETRAP.INFO

SCHOLARSHIP SEARCH UPDATE

For years our organization has fought against scam artists offering phony searches and promising student aid in return for a huge fee. Avoid companies who "guarantee" scholarships or offer to complete the necessary applications for you. Instead try: CollegeAnswer, FastWeb, , SRN Express, ScholarshipExperts, and CollegeBoard.

FEE-BASED SCHOLARSHIP SEARCH

Rarely do we suggest you pay a fee for a scholarship search, but you may wish to check this out. The cost is minimal. To learn more, click on MeritMoney and highlight "About Us" at the top.

SCHOLARSHIPS ONLINE

Students are now able to go online for application details on Nationally recognized scholarships:

American Legion	Americorps	Barry Goldwater
Burger King	Chick-fil-A Leadership	Chick-fil-A WinShape
Coke Interns	Coke Scholars	Collegiate
Gates Millennium Scholars	Harvard University	Hertz Foundation
Intel Science Talent	Jackie Robinson	James Madison Graduate
Kodak	Merck Science Research	Microsoft College Careers
Military Scholarships	Minority Scholarships	Nat'l Defense Grad. Fellowship
National Inventors	National Merit	National Science Foundation
Prudential	Siemens Foundation	The DuPont Challenge
Truman Foundation	Tylenol	Udall Foundation
Wal-Mart	Women Scholarships	Woodrow Wilson Foundation

SCHOLARSHIPS AT PRINCETON

Hats off to one of the country's most prestigious schools. Based on a U.S. News & World Report article, Princeton University will begin using some of its 10.1 billion dollar endowment to fund student scholarships in lieu of burdening students with college loans. To learn more, contact <u>Princeton</u>.

ROTC SCHOLARSHIPS

Hundreds of students will receive ROTC scholarships covering most of their tuition and fees. In addition, the military provides a substantial monthly stipend. There are now more than 55,000 students actively participating in the ROTC program available at 600 colleges and universities across America. For information regarding 2, 3 and 4-year ROTC scholarships, log onto the <u>Army</u>, <u>Navy</u>, or <u>Air Force</u>.

MACY'S PARADE OF SCHOLARSHIPS

Federated Department Stores Foundation has announced a new scholarship program beginning with the graduating high school class of 2008. Federated operates 36 Bloomingdale's department stores and over 800 Macy's nationwide. The program is specifically designed for 54 high school students each year who are children of full-time Federated employees. The program will be administered by the National Merit Scholarship Corporation and the scholarships will be awarded for four years at $1,000 per year.

SCHOLARSHIPS FOR STUDENT-ATHLETES

Former professional athlete, Charlie Kadupski, notes, "If you're serious and want to pursue a college education, there is a program that will fit your academic, athletic, financial and geographic needs." See <u>The Sport Source</u>.

VETERAN'S BENEFITS HIGHLIGHTED

For the brave men and women who have just left the service and are looking for educational benefits, log onto <u>Veterans</u> for updates on college admission, scholarships, and military-friondly schools. In addition, your military training courses and occupational specialty may be considered for college credit. This is a non-government site supported by advertising.

Chapter V

Saving for College

Tuition Payments

Covering the rising cost of a college education can be one of the most challenging assignments parents and students ever face. College tuition fees are due in advance, unlike homes and automobiles that are amortized over a period from 3 to 30 years. Ideally, students and parents should have a savings/investment account to pay for college without any debt. Unfortunately, many people have bought into the idea that Uncle Sam provides cheap money for college and they quit saving. The truth is, there is no cheap money unless you qualify for a non-repayable scholarship or tuition grant.

To meet the challenge, some colleges have enlisted the help of outside organizations to spread the tuition payments over a period of twelve months. Generally, the outside provider makes the heavy tuition payments to the school at the beginning of each quarter or semester, while receiving monthly payments from the parents. In many cases, the plans are interest free but require an annual fee. For detailed information on this procedure, contact the financial aid administrator at the college or university or Facts Management Company, FMC, Tuition Management Systems, TMS, or Tuition Pay.

Some schools have a tuition guarantee plan that guarantees costs will not increase for 2, 3, or even 4 years. Some require a deposit, others a prepayment. Howard Payne University in Brownwood, Texas, guarantees the same tuition costs for all 4 years providing the student remains continuously enrolled and completes twelve credit units per semester.

A college or university may consider a tuition reduction for children of alumni. Some offer a reduced fee for returning adults or 2 or more family members enrolled at the same time. The work-study program may also allow for a tuition reduction. Students should inquire prior to filling out a college application.

Savings Programs

As college costs continue to leap forward, a bleak picture is presented for parents with young children who wish to save for their child's education. By the 2008/09 school year, the overall cost for tuition, room and board, books, and living expenses is expected to reach over $76,000 at a 4-year state school, and over $150,000 at a 4-year private college. The cost for a 4-year undergraduate degree at a state school is projected to climb to nearly $120,000 by 2015.

Savings institutions remained the method of choice for family savings in the past, often sheltered in statement savings accounts. The money remained secure and guaranteed by the Federal Deposit Insurance Corporation (FDIC). The most obvious advantage was accessibility. People could withdraw their money at any time without a penalty. In addition, the institutions paid interest, typically less than the rate of inflation.

During the last decade, many people began to place their savings into other types of interest bearing accounts including Certificates of Deposit, Money Market Accounts, Roth IRA's and the Coverdell Education Savings Accounts.

The interest rate on bank CDs is slightly higher than statement savings; however the money is locked in for the full term of the certificate. There are costly penalties for anyone wanting to withdraw their funds. Both statement savings and Certificates of Deposit are safe and offer little risk. Both are tied to the inflation index which could result in a loss of buying power.

A more flexible method is the money market account available from banks and stock firms. Money market funds are safe, generate higher interest than savings accounts, and can be redeemed at any time without incurring a penalty. They also provide an excellent short-term method for those who want immediate access while earning a more lucrative interest rate.

Many families today are also investing in no-load mutual funds. Mutual funds allow investors to pool their resources with thousands of other investors to buy stock in numerous companies. Each fund has a fund manager who continually moves investors' money to provide the greatest return. While the risk is higher than institutional savings, it is not as risky as purchasing individual bonds or corporate stocks because the money is invested in a wide range of companies.

Coverdell Education Savings Account

The reauthorization of the higher education act in 1997 introduced the Coverdell Education Savings Account, formerly known as the Educational IRA. Families with an Adjusted Gross Income less than $190,000 are eligible to make deposits of $2,000 per year, per child, until the student reaches 18. The earnings are tax-free when used for college tuition, fees, books and room and board. The Coverdell ESA can be rolled over to another member of the family at any time. Once the student reaches age 30, the account must be closed or transferred to a younger member of the family. The ESA can also be used in conjunction with the Hope and the Lifetime Learning education tax credits in the same year. If the funds in the saving account are not used for higher education, they are subject to taxation. (*See Appendix One*)

Interest Compounding

Albert Einstein once acknowledged "Compounding is mankind's greatest invention because it allows for the reliable, systematic accumulation of wealth." It takes but a small amount of money to reach an astonishing gain when the savings are coupled with the power of compounding.

The time value of money and the principle of compounding are powerful concepts. If implemented over the first twenty years of a child's life, this method offers an excellent opportunity to pay for college. The table below illustrates the dynamic effect of interest compounding with an investment of only $50 per month:

Years	Money Invested	5 % Return	10% Return
1	$ 600	$ 614	$ 627
2	1,200	1,258	1,316
3	1,800	1,934	2,075
4	2,400	2,645	2,910
5	3,000	3,391	3,828
6	3,600	4,174	4,838
7	4,200	4,996	5,950
8	4,800	5,860	7,171
9	5,400	6,766	8,515
10	6,000	7,718	9,993
11	6,600	8,718	11,620
12	7,200	9,767	13,409
13	7,800	10,869	15,376
14	8,400	12,026	17,741
15	9,000	13,241	19,922
16	9,600	14,571	22,541
17	10,200	17,263	28,591
19	11,400	18,740	32,078
20	12,000	20,290	35,913

Roth IRA

As a college savings program, the Roth IRA can be a good vehicle for long-term savings. Direct deposits from payroll earnings can be set up and withdrawals can be made without penalty. The main disadvantage is that parents do not earn a tax deduction when contributing to a Roth, verses other IRA's. In many cases, it is more beneficial to contribute to a Roth because the investment earnings generated are sheltered from taxes. Each parent may be eligible to put $4,000 into a Roth IRA every year depending on income. If the parents are over 50 years of age, they each can contribute $5,000 per year.

Uniform Gift to Minors Account

The Uniform Gift to Minors Account (UGMA) custodial program allows parents to select when, where and how their children's savings are invested. With this plan, a custodian is selected, typically the parent, and that custodian makes the investment decisions for the child. When money leaves the account, it must be spent solely for the benefit of the child. Prior to age 18 or 21, depending on the state, the custodian determines the child's spending decisions.

The tax benefits of the UGMA are substantial. As the account grows, the actual earnings on the account are taxed at the child's lower tax rate. If the child is less than 14 years of age, the first $750 of investment income earned by the child each year, i.e., interest, dividends, and capital gains, is totally tax-free. The next $750 of unearned income is taxed at the child's rate, as are all unearned funds for those ages fourteen or older. All unearned income over the initial $1,500 is then taxed at the parent's marginal tax rate. For additional information and updates, parents should contact their tax advisor.

529 PLANS

The fastest growing program in America to help parents with high college tuition costs is the 529 or Qualified State Tuition Plan (named after Section 529 of the IRS Code). "Simply stated, the 529 plan is likely to be your best option for college savings if you have school-age children or grandchildren and are looking to invest significant amounts of money," writes Joseph F. Hurley in, *The Best Way to Save for College*. See Saving for College.

Most state programs allow contributions in one lump sum annually or on a monthly basis. Under Section 529, there are 2 types of programs: 1) State prepaid tuition plans that guarantee the plan will cover future tuition costs at all state colleges and universities; and 2) State college savings plans that do not give the same guarantee but offer a potentially higher rate of return. Not everyone agrees on which part of the plan is the best. See Grade Your 529 Plan.

Both programs allow the student to use the proceeds for tuition and other educational expenses such as room and board. A significant drawback for most state prepaid tuition programs is the loss of the tuition guarantee if a student selects a private college or an out of state school. (Check with the college admissions office.)

Neither plan guarantees admission, but they do allow the family to defer federal taxation on the growth of their investment until the student matriculates. The student then pays federal tax at his or her lower tax rate on the increased value of the education received. Most state programs grant state tax exemption to their residents, and some allow a deduction for the prepaid amounts.

Money magazine columnist, Lani Luciano, writes, "You prepay tuition for the number of years or courses you desire either in a lump sum or in monthly installments. When college rolls around, the value of credits in your state college system is all paid up. Whether a prepaid plan turns out to be a wise investment will depend on how quickly tuition rises in your state and whether and where your kid attends college."

The most frequently asked questions are, "What about a refund should a student decide not to attend college, or elect to attend a college in another state, or move out of state prior to the fulfillment of the plan?"

All programs vary in their refund policy as well as their initial investment procedure. Some states only return the original investment while others refund the principal plus interest. The State of Tennessee offers no refund before the student reaches the age of eighteen. After that, the refund equals the principal plus 50 percent of the increase.

The newest Prepaid Tuition Plan managed by TIAA-CREF basically sells shares that represent a fixed percentage of a year's tuition for 240 private institutions. Everyone pays the same for the shares. Log on to Tuition Plan for more information regarding the specialized "Independent 529 Plan."

Chapter VI

Money Management

The Basics

As previous stated, the role of paying for college has shifted from the parents to the student. As a result, more students are opting for student loans than ever before. Today over 60 percent of all financial aid is government-backed student or parent loans. As tuition costs continue to rise out of control, student borrowing continues to escalate to over $40 billion.

No matter how little or how much you and your family have invested or saved, money management is essential. In order to survive in college, you need to manage your money and avoid long-term debt. To graduate with the least amount of debt, it is critical that you maintain complete control of your spending. The best way to accomplish this goal is to have a well-thought-out spending plan. Basically a spending plan, or budget, is nothing more than a financial guide to help you meet your needs without going into debt. Like a road map, a spending plan can help you see where you're going as well as where you have been. (*See Appendix Two for a budget example and helpful budget worksheets.*)

After graduation, students are tempted to buy some of the necessities they were deprived of in college, such as a new sofa that's not stained and broken from years of abuse, or the latest megawatt home theatre system, or a washer and dryer that runs without quarters. True, these are important, but you should always rely on your spending plan to determine ways to purchase the items with cash before signing on the dotted line for 36 months of payments. One student graduated with an MBA in business, yet never learned the basics of *"personal"* money management. As a result, he soon became bogged down with car payments, house payments, furniture payments, student loan payments, and high credit card payments. Since he did not have a spending plan in place, he ended up entrapped in financial bondage for years.

Spending Plan Formula

For planning purposes, the following formula, i.e., TAF minus T&T = NSI, is easy to use and highly versatile. More importantly, the plan will help you track your spending and develop proper spending habits prior to graduation.

TAF, or Total Available Funds, embraces all incoming finances from all sources regardless of the amount, including money from parents, aunts, uncles, savings accounts, college loans, student employment, grants, and scholarships.

T&T means Taxes and Tithe. Although you may not pay taxes while in school, taxes will play an important role in the management of your income following graduation. The second "T" is for tithe, offering a portion of your earnings to a place of worship. Once you've noted all incoming finances and deducted applicable tithe and taxes, the remaining is entitled NSI.

NSI means Net Spendable Income. This is the money you have available for housing, food, books, tuition, travel, and every other conceivable expense known to students worldwide.

To properly execute your spending plan, list all the items you plan to purchase with the remaining funds. Some of the expenditures will fall under a category known as "fixed" expenses, or those items that remain virtually the same each month. Examples may include rent, tuition, car payments and car insurance.

"Variable" expenses such as food, clothing, entertainment, utilities, money for unexpected repairs, or gifts are extremely difficult to budget. Although a challenge, you can make it work simply by using the sample budget forms included here.

The college-spending plan has suggested categories and accompanying worksheets for you to use as a guide. The figures to post in each category are your figures and the allocation of the funds should be given serious consideration. If you allocated 3/4ths of all available funds on food, very little would be left for books, clothes, oil changes, etc.

By seeking wise counsel, tracking expenses, eliminating impulsive buying, avoiding high interest loans, and spending based on your spending plan, not your checkbook, you can shun financial bondage whether you're single or a married student seeking to graduate debt free.

NOTE: The key to success for any spending plan is to maintain flexibility. As your needs change, move your funds from one category to another. You may allocate money into one category and later find it is more than necessary. At that point, some of the dollars can be moved to another category that may be running short. By keeping the spending plan up-to-date and flexible, you will know at a glance how much money is available and avoid overspending. (*See Appendix Two*)

The Credit Card Ambush

Robert Bugai, President of the New Jersey based College Marketing Intelligence, notes that many students fill out credit card applications as soon as they arrive on campus. "The financial services industry probably outspends all others when it comes to campus promotions."

Bookstores will often have a table set up with credit card applications along with a choice of free gifts. "The free gifts are used as a hook to get students to apply," said Bugai. "The problem is that students can apply ten times and each time, receive another free gift."

Most credit card companies are eager to have students use their cards for cash withdrawals. The reason is simple. At the moment of withdrawal, the bank collects a 2 percent service charge plus the usual high interest rate from that day forward.

With so much credit available to students, it comes as no surprise that many are in financial trouble before graduation. If a student goes on a credit card binge and is unable to make the required payments, he or she will end up with poor credit and may have problems getting a job, attending graduate school or renting an apartment. Bugai also notes that it's not uncommon for students to declare bankruptcy

Technically speaking, the credit card is an incredible advancement in the world of finances. The ease and simplicity of the system is amazing. If a person carries a major credit card such as a VISA®, MasterCard® or American Express®, there is little need for currency whether in a restaurant in Iowa City, Maui or Bangkok. Using your credit card for gasoline, clothes, and nice restaurants is not wrong. It is simply the misuse of your credit cards that will eventually come back to haunt you.

In her book, *The Ultimate Credit Handbook*, author and speaker, Gerri Detweiler, says, "A credit card is nothing more than a means of accessing a personal loan, but because of the glitzy advertising, few people think of a card that way. Instead we think of credit cards as a means of convenience, a shortcut to the 'good life,' symbols of financial success, or even an extension of our income."

> *"A credit card is nothing more than a means of accessing a personal loan."*

Detweiler adds that college students are big targets for the lending institutions. In their zeal to capture the college market, credit card companies spend millions of dollars each year promoting their cards on campus. In many cases, the bank's only requirement is a student ID. "Even without any established credit, lenders are eager to capture their loyalty along with their pocketbook. Each year banks lure unsuspecting students with special promotions such as no annual fee, gold cards, titanium cards, frequent flyer miles, special discounts on new cars, and other incentives. Citibank easily leads the pack as the top college card issuer," writes Detweiler. "Their applications litter the dormitories and classrooms of every campus in America, and they're easy to get. Unfortunately, most of the major credit cards offered through the college enlistment programs carry high interest rates."

When addressing students on the subject of credit, Detweiler references the minimum payment syndrome as a very clever means contrived by the banks to make lots of money. As an example of how this works, she explains, "If a [student] has a balance of $1,000 on a credit card with an annual fee of $20 at a interest rate of nearly 20 percent and chooses to pay only the minimum of 3 percent of the unpaid balance each month, it will take 8 years to pay the debt, cost $843 in finance charges and $180 dollars in membership fees for a total of $2023."

One college student began collecting credit cards as a status symbol. By his 20th birthday, he had amassed some eighteen gasoline and department store cards, 5 VISA® Gold cards, 5 MasterCard's®, one American Express® card and some $17,000 of debt. As the pressure for payment increased, he borrowed funds from one card to pay the minimum on another. He had become a slave to the lenders. He was basically caught in the credit card trap.

Are the banks that offer the credit cards to blame? No, not directly. The cards are not the problem. It's the misuse of the cards that plagues everyone, including many college students.

Most banks portray an image of solidarity with their customers and promote their interest free grace period. The truth is, if you opt to pay just the minimum, *there is no grace period!* Once a minimum payment is sent to a bank, the grace period is canceled. From that point on, you're charged the maximum interest rate from the moment you use the card until the balance is paid in full. For many students, once caught in the trap, it's almost impossible to escape.

Our society breeds on credit and credit cards and consumer credit accounts are available to nearly everyone. One young college graduate found the ease of acquiring credit cards led directly to excessive spending and thousands of dollars of debt. Eventually she turned to a nationally recognized nonprofit organization called Consumer Credit Counseling Service who worked out a plan to repay all her creditors and restore her damaged credit score. For more information and the nearest CCCS location, students may call 800-388-2227.

Best Use of a Credit Card

a. Open just one credit card account while in school.

b. Use the card sparingly and only when you have the funds available to pay off the card when the bill arrives.

c. Avoid paying the minimum amount. Always pay the entire amount to avoid heavy finance charges.

d. Shop for a credit card with no annual fee and a 25-day grace period. Note: *There is no grace period on future purchases unless the bill is fully paid each month.*

e. Be weary of the low-interest "come-on rates" promised by the banks. The banks are permitted by law to change the interest rates with only a 2-week written notice to cardholders, regardless of the promises posted on the advertising flyers and envelopes.

f. Report any lost or stolen cards to the bank within 48 hours which will limit your liability to $50 in unauthorized charges. If you're not aware of the loss immediately and fail to report it to the bank within the designated time, you may be held liable for up to $500 in fraudulent charges.

Other Entrapments

There are many other opportunities waiting just around the corner on every campus for the unsuspecting student. Consider the Rent to Own rip-off. Occasionally roommates will collectively pick out new furniture for their college apartment at one of the rent-to-own stores. College apartments often receive very harsh treatment. What seems like a minor decision can later produce major headaches and horrendous user fees, often higher than the cost of the furniture if purchased at retail. College students should avoid furniture rental stores and shop instead at neighborhood garage sales and used furniture outlets. The Salvation Army and Goodwill stores often have used furniture available.

Still another (and perhaps the most dangerous of all) is the infamous Lottery. Research supports the claim that very few lottery winners are ever found financially ahead after their winnings. In most cases, the result of winning a lottery is disastrous. The man who won the largest single jackpot ($314.9 million) has been arrested multiple times including drunken driving and assault. Less than two years after he cashed in the giant purse, his granddaughter's friend was found dead. Shortly thereafter, the same granddaughter was found dead from an apparent drug overdose. When interviewed by the local newspaper, his wife said, "I wish all of this never would have happened. I wish I had torn the ticket up."

A young Georgia winner who pocketed $20 million recently declared bankruptcy, two divorces later and $5 million dollars in debt. A Pennsylvania lottery winner now lives off government welfare after winning his $16.2 million. One lady won $18 million but ended up with only $700 left in two bank accounts after enjoying her winnings that led to bankruptcy. Report after report reads much the same. The single most obvious failure in every case is the lack of financial management.

As a college student, you can learn from others failures and avoid the lottery ticket lines. By managing your money while attending college and after graduation, you'll experience financial freedom far in excess of one of the "get rich quick" schemes.

Car Purchases

One fundamental purchase you will face someday is budgeting for a new automobile. Because most new automobiles lose up to 35 percent of their value in the first year, it makes good economic sense to shop for a quality used car or off-lease vehicle.

Tom Wells, a financial seminar instructor for Crown Financial Ministries (Crown), developed a classic value vs. cost chart. The chart illustrates that the most cost-effective period to purchase a vehicle is when the car is between 3 and 4 years old. Comparing depreciation and life expectancy, it's at that point where the cost of the automobile vs. the vehicle's value reaches an optimum.

Leasing products has been around for many decades, but it was not until the 1980's that auto leasing took on a new dimension. Saddled with massive inventories, the automobile manufacturers found that consumers would respond in great numbers when offered a manufacturer's rebate or special leasing incentive. In most cases, consumers end up paying more when leasing an automobile than when they purchase, with nothing to show for it at the end of the term. This method of doing business has carried forward to this day and promises to be a major player in all areas of business during the 21st century. Except in business situations, or for the person who easily budgets for a new automobile every 2 years, automobile leasing is not recommended.

Balancing a Checkbook

By the time students graduate from high school, most are familiar with a checking account, yet many end up paying exorbitant bank fees while in college. Where students fail is simply in basic record keeping. Once you open a new account, the bank will send you regular statements itemizing all the transactions that have occurred in the previous month.

We recommend you order duplicate checks from the bank so you will always have a copy of every check written and avoid the possibility of forgetting to post an entry. Save all ATM and debit card receipts and subtract each amount from the checkbook balance on a daily basis.

To cover costs, most banks add a monthly service charge. Since the charges vary from bank to bank, shop around for the best plan. Of course, these charges also need to be added into the checkbook register in order to maintain a proper balance.

Balancing a checking account once a month is simply a matter of perseverance and patience. Ultimately, your checkbook will balance with the monthly bank statement and provide an ample historical record of your major expenditures.

If you follow the 5 steps shown here, you'll balance your checking account and avoid most bank charges:

STEP ONE: The first step in balancing a checkbook is to note which checks have been paid by the bank. Place a mark in your checkbook register next to each check indicated on the bank statement. Cross them off the statement as well.

STEP TWO: This step compares all ATM and check card receipts with the bank statement. Follow the same procedure by marking off each debit in both the checkbook register and statement.

STEP THREE: Next, if the statement does not list any outstanding checks or recent ATM and check card transactions, list each of those on the back and total the column.

STEP FOUR: Step Four is the same as the previous step, except you list all the deposits not shown on the bank statement. If the statement does not indicate your recent deposits, these need to be noted on the back of the statement page as well and totaled.

STEP FIVE: The final step is simply to perform the required calculations. Add the total deposits from Step Four to the statement balance and deduct the total outstanding items from Step Three. That will give you your true balance. If that figure matches your checkbook register, your account is balanced and needs no additional attention. If you're unable to balance your account, don't be afraid to ask the trained professionals at their local bank branch for assistance.

Check Cards

Many students carry a debit check card with a VISA® or MasterCard® logo. While it looks and acts much like a credit card, a check card is basically an electronic check and can be used by anyone wherever a credit card is accepted. Since the money is deducted directly from the bank, a thief could clear out your entire checking account in a matter of minutes. If you have a Visa® or MasterCard® check card, use it cautiously.

If your check card is lost or stolen, the risk to you is the same as with a credit card. If the bank is notified within the allotted 48 hours, the bank will hold you responsible for only $50 in charges. If the bank is not notified within 48 hours, the bank can hold you responsible for up to $500 in unauthorized charges.

ATM Debit Cards

Like the check card above, the ATM card is also a debit card, but without a VISA® or MasterCard® logo. Today many retailers allow you to use your debit card for purchases as well as for additional cash. The key difference between the check card and the ATM card is the requirement to add a "pin" number for each withdrawal or purchase, thus assuring privacy and security. One note of advice: Request money from an ATM machine owned by the issuing bank to avoid fees charged by other banks and merchants who own and operate ATM machines inside their business.

AVOIDING FINANCIAL BONDAGE

NOTE: ALL INTERNET LINKS IN *TheCollegeTrap* ARE UNDERLINED.
TO ACTIVATE THE WEB LINKS, GO TO WWW.THECOLLEGETRAP.INFO

STUDENT LOAN PLAGUE

Students are allowed to borrow up to $138,500 in government-backed loans without any known source of income or credit. Today, many ask themselves, "Is it worth it?" A recent survey found that 54 percent said they would borrow less if they had to do it over again. Read the full article in Money Matters.

SPENDING PLANS AVOID STUDENT DEBT

A well-thought-out spending plan, or budget, is critical for students wanting to graduate with the least amount of debt. Writing for Nellie Mae, Kathleen Gibbons notes that, "A budget (the noun) is simply a list of your resources, minus your expenses, generally recorded on a monthly basis. But budgeting (the verb) is something more. The act of budgeting also means identifying goals, such as saving for a vacation over spring break, or buying a *used* car, or simply having enough money to pay your bills and have pizza money every weekend, and making adjustments as needed to help meet your goals." Click on Trials and Triumphs.

STUDENT LOANS AND YOU?

Writing for Boundless Webzine, author Heather Koerner paints a remarkably clear picture of what it's like when colleges offer student loans so freely, which invariably end up not so free after graduation. See the full article at Count the Cost.

TIPS ON CUTTING COLLEGE COSTS

High school students should read the following article on how to reduce the overall cost of attending college. Check out Crosswalk.

COLLEGE FUNDING

To view an article on college finances originally published in Larry Burkett's Money Matters, click on College Funding. This is a PDF file. If the file fails to open, download Acrobat Reader, free from Adobe.

CREDIT CARD DEBT STALKS STUDENTS

"University students are amassing record amounts of debt on credit cards," writes Mark Helm of the Hearst Newspapers. "...many young people will be spending their earnings paying off debt at the very time they should be socking away money for their future." Log onto Student Debt. See a new research report from Nellie Mae.

Chapter VII

Alternative Funding

Co-op Programs

As tuition and fees continue to climb, some students are opting for the cooperative education program available at over 700 colleges and universities throughout the United States. It is estimated that nearly 300,000 students participate in college co-op programs and earn as much as $14,000 to $16,000 each year.

The main educational advantage of a cooperative program is that classroom theory is tirelessly tested in the workplace. This encourages students toward a strong work ethic and helps develop workers who can translate theory into action.

As a way of testimony, this author held multiple jobs during college working as a dishwasher in a student dormitory, retail sales in a men's store, selling newspaper advertising, and managing a newspaper circulation department. At one time the author attended classes every morning dressed in a business suit prior to working at a large international advertising agency in the heart of San Francisco.

The co-op plan is also helpful in establishing roots within the business community. Those who attend college for one quarter followed by a quarter of work often stay with the same employer after graduation. Some programs allow students to attend school during the fall and spring quarters and work during the winter and summer periods. Co-op programs can be found in 3 different types:

- The **AM/PM Plan** - Work in the morning and attend classes every afternoon, or the opposite.
- The **Day/Night Plan** - Work a full schedule during the day and attend classes at night.
- The **50/50 Plan** - work one quarter; attend school one quarter.

Some colleges have their own co-op programs providing a nearly free college education for those willing to work on campus. For more on this, check out Alice Lloyd College, Berea College, College of the Ozarks, Blackburn College, Sterling College, and Warren Wilson College at Work Colleges. Imagine graduating from college with little or no debt to hold you back from fulfilling all your dreams. Only a few students are accepted each year at Deep Springs College in California, but those who make the grade never look back, and often go on to some of the nation's elite universities.

Federal Co-op

The federal government hires bright college students to keep the agencies running smoothly and offers the widest choice of work sites, academic opportunities and career fields through Student Educational Employment Program (SEEP). The SEEP program is open to all undergraduates as well as graduate and Ph.D. candidates. Students should contact the office for co-op education at their college, or call the Federal Employment Information Center listed in the phone directory.

Eligible SEEP students can work one half day and attend classes one half day, or alternate a quarter or semester of school with a quarter or semester of work. Normally, a cooperative education program will add one year to a student's enrollment.

Americorps

In exchange for ten months of full-time service, Uncle Sam will provide students an education award of $4,725 to be used for technical training or college tuition through the Americorps program. Participants also receive housing, uniforms, a living stipend and a weekly food allowance.

Members serve in teams of 10 to 15 and live on one of 5 Americorps campuses in the United States. Ventures may include setting up a new 911 system, leading a childhood literacy program, providing living assistance to the elderly, fighting forest fires, providing disaster relief and many other interesting projects. Skills for specific projects are taught before members begin their community efforts. Training in leadership, team building, citizenship and physical conditioning is provided. Americorps is open to all young adults ages 18 to 24. For more information, contact Americorps at 800-942-2677 or on the Internet at Americorps.

Avoiding Debt

Perhaps the number one way is to graduate without a millstone of debt around your neck and avoid student loans is to select a college or university that best fits your academic achievements, national test scores, grade point average, and your family's budget. Compare your academic prowess with other incoming students at a particular institution. If you appear average at one college but far above average at another, the second school is more likely to offer early acceptance and institutional scholarships.

Advanced Placement®

Advanced Placement (AP®) classes are college-level courses available to high school students. According to the College Board, there are now 35 different <u>AP classes</u> covering 20 key subject areas, although not every subject is available in every school. Advanced Placement classes can be helpful to you. Here's why:

1. Admissions committees view students with several advanced placement classes in a favorable light.
2. Students who pass the optional Advanced Placement Examination at the completion of the class may earn college credits.
3. Students who earn college credits for their AP® classes save hundreds of dollars by reducing the number of semesters or quarters   needed for graduation.
4. There are over 1,400 colleges and universities in America that will issue sophomore standing to an incoming student who has successfully passed the number of AP® classes the institution requires.

Advanced placement classes enable you to earn a grade higher than your overall scores. In other words, a high school student who earns a B in an advanced placement class scores a 4-point. A grade of A is posted as a 5-point. This type of scoring is known as a weighted score, resulting in a weighted GPA. Some colleges still prefer only non-weighted scores when determining scholarship awards.

Company Paid Tuition   - UPS job

As previously noted, this is one of the most over-stated examples of unused scholarship money, and is often one of the figures used by unscrupulous companies to lure people into their scholarship search scam.

The Company Tuition Plan is not available to every student. Only employees who work for an employer willing to pay for them to return to college are eligible. These are private funds and should not be mistaken as unused student financial aid dollars.

For those that do qualify, up to $5,250 may be used for tuition, books and travel. The fees paid by the employer are taxable. All other expenses may be deducted on Schedule A, Form 1040, when filing federal income taxes. Internal Revenue Service rules change frequently and participants in this plan should consult their company personnel office for changes.

8 Alternative Ways to Pay for College (by Lucy Lazarony)
Source: Bankrate.com, N. Palm Beach, FL 2006.

The news on college costs is mighty grim, but there are plenty of creative ways to keep your college dream on track. Dwindling state and federal aid, lower endowments and drops in fund raising have forced many colleges and universities to raise tuition prices and cut back on financial aid programs. What's a cash-strapped student to do? First off, face facts -- These are trying times for anyone pursuing higher education. It's time to pull out all the stops. Be flexible. Be determined. Be willing to give the unusual a try. Here's a roundup of some offbeat and overlooked strategies for pursuing and paying for a college degree.

1. Accelerate your degree

Accelerated classes cram a semester's worth of material into 6 or 8-week sessions. The classes, while intense, can really help to move up your graduation date. You land the degree you want at a much lower price.

Tuition in an accelerated degree program at Albert Magnus College in New Haven, Conn., is about half of the cost of its traditional degree program. And many schools offer bachelor's degree programs in 3 years instead of 4.

For students on the physician track, George Washington University in Washington, D.C., offers a 7-year program integrating a bachelor's degree with a medical degree, saving a full year's costs. At Seton Hill College in Greensburg, Pennsylvania., a student can receive a bachelor's degree and a master's degree in elementary art education for the price of a bachelor's degree. An accelerated degree program is a great option for a student with a clear career goal. If you're ready to work hard, why not put your college education on the fast track?

2. Be a transfer student

In many cases, credits earned at a less-expensive college or university can be transferred and applied toward a degree from a pricey, elite school. You could earn a prestigious diploma at a fraction of the price. So why not attend a community college for a couple of years and then transfer to your dream college? It's not as if the fancy diploma you'll hang on your wall will say "transfer student."

Taking the transfer-student route will save you some serious cash. Every credit earned at a low-cost community college could save you hundreds of dollars in tuition. Also, by bunking at your parent's house, you could knock down your room-and-board charges to zero.

"You get some of your core curriculum out of the way for a cheaper price," says David Cooper, who runs the college-bound Web site Wiredscholar at www.salliemae.com.

The first step is learning about articulation agreements at your dream university and nearby 2-year colleges. An articulation agreement specifies which community college course credits will be accepted toward a bachelor's degree at the 4-year college or university. It also outlines scholarship requirements and specifies what kind of grades a student must achieve to transfer to the 4-year school as a junior.

3. Go where you're wanted

Somewhere out there is a college or university that's dying to have you as a student. Find that school, fire off an application and watch the cost of your college education drop. "Every student is a star at the right college," says Ray Loewe, president of College Money, a financial planning firm in Marlton, New Jersey, specializing in helping parents pay for college. And star students get deep discounts for their education. A college that really wants you will find the aid and scholarships to keep you. "Colleges know what they want, and if you fit their criteria, they're willing to pay." The trick is finding the school that considers you a star.

Peruse college guides. Do your grades and SAT® scores match or exceed the average marks of the current student body? Does the college offer the courses you want? If so, this could be the school that rolls out the red carpet for you. "Choose a college where you fit in the top 25 to 30 percent of a class," Loewe says. "Obviously, the higher you are the more the school wants you and the better position you're in." Not sure where to start your college search? Begin by checking out smaller, regional colleges in your area. An excellent but less-known college may be searching for a student like you.

4. Choose a tuition-free school

Overwhelmed by tuition prices and the prospect of paying massive student loans after you graduate? Why not attend a tuition-free school? You get the college education you want without the hefty price tag. The catch? You may have to work. Some schools require students to work 10 to 15 hours a week on campus and in jobs related to their majors. Tuition-free colleges include The Cooper Union in New York, New York; Webb Institute in Glen Cove, New York; Berea College in Berea, Kentucky.; College of the Ozarks in Point Lookout, Missouri.; and Alice Lloyd College in Pippa Passes, Kentucky. (See Work Colleges)

5. Get a sponsor

Can't quite swing the cost of college? Get a little help from a rich uncle. MyRichUncle provides money from private investors to college students who need help with education expenses. In return, a student agrees to pay a fixed percentage of their gross future income for a fixed period. "They pay less when they make less," says Raza Khan, managing director of MyRichUncle. "They pay more when they make more." This is an education investment not a loan, so there's no interest to pay. For every $1,000 of financial help, a student agrees to pay 10 to 40 basis points of future income. A basis point is one one-hundredth of a percentage point, so someone who receives an education investment of $10,000 might agree to pay anywhere from 1 to 4 percent of future income. Payment periods are 10 years for graduate students and 15 years for undergraduate students. Payments begin 6 months after graduation. Once the payment period ends, a student's obligation ends even if you end up paying back less than you were given. "We're actually taking a chance on a student," Khan says. "If a student succeeds, we succeed."

6. Lock in tuition

Can't stand the way college tuition keeps shooting up? Consider locking in a single-tuition rate for 4 years. The tuition rate you pay as a wet-behind-the-ears freshman is guaranteed until you graduate. No more losing sleep over tuition costs.

Colleges with locked-in tuition programs include Anna Maria College in Paxton, Massachusetts.; Baylor University in Waco, Texas; Centenary College of Louisiana in Shreveport, Louisiana.; Concordia University in River Forest, Illinois.; Hardin-Simmons University in Abilene, Texas; Huntington College in Huntington, Indiana.; Urbana University in Urbana, Ohio; the University of Charleston in Charleston, West Virginia.; and New York's Pace University. Some schools charge a fee for the program.

7. Never give up on scholarships

You don't have to be a stellar student to land a big scholarship. Unless it's strictly an academic scholarship, your grades don't really matter. As long as your grades make the cutoff, often a 2.5 GPA or higher, you have as good a chance as any applicant of bagging a scholarship. And there's no reason your scholarship search can't continue through 4 years of college. "It's really just beating the bushes," Cooper says.

The Web is a great way to get started. Check out individual college Web sites, and search for scholarship sources on FastWeb, ScholarshipCoach.com, and College Board. Avoid web sites that charge you to search for scholarships.

Don't overlook local sources of scholarships. Community-based awards may be smaller, but they're also easier to win. "Students should look to organizations such as the Kiwanis Club, YMCA, parents' employers and area businesses." You can learn about local competitions at the public library and at the guidance office at your local high school.

8. Work off debt with community service

Got your degree? Why not do some good and wipe out a big chunk of education debt at the same time? Recent college grads can cancel part or all of their federal-education debt by working in public-service jobs -- lower-paying professional jobs that serve low-income communities -- or by volunteering. Loan-forgiveness programs are available to everyone from teachers to nurses to young doctors and lawyers to Peace Corps volunteers. Teachers who work in low-income elementary or secondary schools may be able to cancel as much as $17,500 of their federal Stafford loan debt.

Other Co-op Programs

The National Health Service Corps offers loan-forgiveness programs to physicians, nurse practitioners, physician assistants, midwives, dentists, dental hygienists, psychologists and therapists who work for 2 years in communities in great need of health professionals.

Several volunteer organizations also provide assistance with student loan debt. Peace Corps volunteers who complete a 2-year term can wipe out 30 percent of their Perkins loan balance. Student loan payments may also be deferred while serving in the Peace Corps.

Members of VISTA receive educational awards of $4,725 for each year of service. These awards can be applied to student loans or future education expenses.

ALTERNATIVE FUNDING IDEAS

NOTE: ALL INTERNET LINKS IN *TheCollegeTrap* ARE UNDERLINED.
TO ACTIVATE THE WEB LINKS, GO TO WWW.THECOLLEGETRAP.INFO

CLEP TESTS CAN SAVE STUDENTS THOUSANDS

The College-Level Examination Program® or CLEP®, allows students to earn college credit for what they already know. The College Board has a special web site just for CLEP.

CREDIT BY EXAM

For those returning to college after a hiatus, one web site has an extended number of links to testing programs including CLEP, DANTES, and Advanced Placement, making it possible to accelerate your degree. For more on this, check out Back to College.

START COLLEGE AS A SOPHOMORE

The surge in the number of students taking AP tests is changing America's schools. Nearly 2 million students recently took AP exams, a whopping increase over the number of the college-level tests taken a decade ago. "The Advanced Placement Program, which began as a tiny experiment for top seniors seeking college courses and credit, has swelled to the point of altering the high school experience," notes Ben Feller at the Associated Press. "A few hundred public high schools used to offer AP; now two-thirds of them do." High scores on Advanced Placement exams can save thousands of dollars by enabling students to enter college with sophomore status. For more information, click on AP Classes.

INCREDIBLE LOAN PAYBACK PROGRAM

The Office of Personnel Management (OPM) in Washington reports an increase in the number of students taking advantage of their student loan payback. Basically the program is used to recruit or retain highly qualified personnel for government agencies. Each agency is authorized under 5 U.S.C. 5379 to offer the program to qualified employees, whether graduated or not. The agencies are allowed to pay back $10,000 in student loans per year up to a maximum of $60,000. What's the catch? First of all there is no guarantee that you will automatically qualify for the program. The loan payback program is part of the up front employment recruiting process that you negotiate. Secondly, you must remain with the government for a minimum of 3 years. If you leave ahead of that, you're required to reimburse OPM for the total amount of the loan payback. Thirdly, the payback is taxable and the $10,000 will be taxed as ordinary income. Make sure you get everything in writing. For more information, click on Questions & Answers.

NATIONAL COMMISSION FOR COOPERATIVE ED

80 percent of the top Fortune 500 companies employ co-op students according to the National Co-op Commission. Students may earn as much as $14,000 to $18,000 annually through a college co-op program. One of the best co-op programs or summer employment opportunities can be found at the NSA web site. Once there, scroll down to "Student Programs." Finally, click on "Cooperative Education Program."

BOOMING DISTANCE EDUCATION

As distance education continues to grow, students are now able to earn their Bachelor's or Master's Degree on their home computer at virtual schools like JIU and UofP, or online with UMUC, Moody or Liberty. For an updated list of schools offering online degrees, log onto ClassesUSA. One word of caution; be sure the school you choose is truly accredited by CHEA.

529 INVESTMENT FUNDS

A 529 Plan may be a family's best investment tool to offset the increasing cost of college. It is also a great place for parents or grandparents to add to a student's college savings account without the usual tax consequences. For more information and new savings plans, check out 529 Plans, Comparative Plans, Enterprise, College Savings and Vanguard.

Chapter VIII

Military Options

Selecting one of the military options provides every student the opportunity to graduate from college without being entrapped with thousands of dollars in student loans.

ROTC Scholarships

Two, 3 and 4-year scholarships are available for undergraduates at hundreds of schools across the country through the Reserve Officers' Training Corps. For a service obligation of 4 to 8 years, the benefits include tuition fees up to $20,000 per year, all books, and a monthly stipend of $400 or more per month. Officer candidates attend 6 weeks of training between their sophomore and junior years in college, and 6 weeks of advanced training between their junior and senior years. Depending on the service, graduates begin their assignment as an Ensign or Second Lieutenant. Students already enrolled in college may also apply for 2 or 3 year scholarships. Requirements include:

- A good high school transcript
- Excellent physical condition
- Weight proportionate with height
- The approval of the Scholarship Acceptance Board
- Upper 10-20 percent of your class
- Have an interest in science or engineering
- Score above average on the SAT® or ACT®

If you do not qualify for a scholarship but are accepted into the advanced ROTC program at your college, you will receive a stipend of $150 or more per month beginning in your junior year, plus regular service pay for the summer training camps, and a military commission as an Ensign or Second Lieutenant.

Applications are time-sensitive. Students must apply in the fall of their senior year. Contact the college ROTC department or go online to Army, Navy, Air Force, Marines.

Loan Repayment Program

The Army and Navy have a loan repayment program for those who have already attended college and are burdened with excessive student loans, whether graduated or not.

Assuming the loans are not in default, the Army will pay back up to $65,000 in Perkins, PLUS and Stafford Loans in return for a   3-year commitment as an enlisted member. If the student has already graduated, he or she would begin military service with the rank of E-4 and earn an additional $500 or more per month. Once the 3-year enlistment is completed, graduates may be eligible for Officer Candidate School.

College graduates employed in a <u>nonmilitary</u> position would find it difficult to pay back $65,000 in school loans in just 3 years. Even if new job paid $50,000 per year, there would only be $15,659 left to live on to cover entertainment, food, car payment, insurance, and rent, after the heavy loan payments and all the taxes are deducted.

The following example is based upon estimated tax calculations for a single person committed to paying back $65,000 in student loans at the rate of $21,666 per year for 3 years:

Income less:	Federal	State	Social	= Take Home	less Loan Payback	= Balance
$30M	($2,900)	($1,050)	($2,295)	$23,755	($21,666)	$ 2,089
$40M	($4,600)	($1,450)	($3,060)	$30,890	($21,666)	$ 9,224
$50M	($7,100)	($1,750)	($3,825)	$37,325	($21,666)	$15,659
$70M	($12,100)	($2,450)	($5,355)	$50,095	($21,666)	$28,429

GI Bill and Select Programs

Every military branch has enlistment quotas and tools to assist their recruiting efforts. In place of the College Fund, the Army can offer an incoming recruit $12,000 as an enlistment bonus for specific job specialties plus the Montgomery GI Bill. For more information, call 800-USAArmy or check out www.goarmy.com.

The 'pro-college' Montgomery GI Bill is available for every enlisted person in the military, regardless of the branch of service. When servicemen and women allocate $100 per month into an educational fund for the first 12 months of service, the government will add a sizeable amount of money to the original $1,200 investment.

For a 4-year enlistment, the Army, Marine Corps, Air Force, Coast

Guard and Navy add $36,000 to the initial $1,200 for a total of $37,200 in benefits through the Montgomery GI Bill. Once out of the service, the veteran will have up to $1034 per month for 36 months to use for any trade school, flight school or college in America.

When applicants are accepted into the Navy's prestigious nuclear power program, they will receive $70,000 or more in cash benefits for college for a 6-year commitment, and an opportunity to earn an Associate degree before leaving the service. The Navy also pays up to 75 percent of any additional tuition costs while the servicemen and women are on active duty.

To qualify for the nuclear power program, applicants must hold a certified diploma from an accredited high school, have a strong math and science background, be drug free, and pass the Navy Advanced Program Test. There are many opportunities available in the missile technical field aboard submarines, and aboard the Navy's newest nuclear-powered aircraft carriers.

The Navy Department has a plan to help servicemen and women remain debt free while earning their Associate's or Bachelor's Degree. The Navy College Assistance program is essentially a delayed entry program where students attend the college of their choice for 12 months at the Navy's expense (up to $18,000) prior to entering active service. Students must agree to successfully complete at least one college level algebra class and one physics-based science course while maintaining a 2.5 or above GPA.

After the 12 month period, students report for basic training. Upon completion of basic, students transfer to the Navy's Nuclear Propulsion School where they receive 2 years of highly technical training, much of which is transferable for college credit. Those interested can go online at www.navyjobs.com or call 800-872-6289.

For a 3-year commitment, the Air Force adds $36,000 to the initial

$1,200 for a total of $37,200 in benefits through the Montgomery GI Bill. Active duty men and women can earn their Associate's degree through the accredited Community College of the Air Force with the military paying up to 75 percent of all tuition costs.

High school graduates entering the Army may apply for admission into a college or university through the Army Concurrent Admissions Program (ConAP). The Army will pay 75 percent of tuition costs. If the candidate meets all the requirements for admission into one of the ConAP colleges, he or she will receive a written admission guarantee and be assigned a special college academic advisor. Men and women can earn college credits while on active duty, later transferable to that college. Participating in the plan can save thousands of dollars by shortening the time needed to graduate.

College Fund

Those who serve in a critical job area are eligible for the Army and Navy's impressive College Fund, now up to $71,000.

Time	Initial Savings	+ GI Bill	+ College Fund	= Per Month	Total
2 years	$1,200	$29,000	$ 5,400	$ 988	$35,600
3 years	$1,200	$36,000	$16,200	$1,483	$53,400
4 years	$1,200	$36,000	$30,600	$1,883	$67,800
6 years	$1,200	$36,000	$34,200	$1,977	$71,200

With the college fund, students who serve 4 years in the military will receive $67,800 or nearly $1,900 each month for 36 months to attend a college of their choice. The only requirement to be part of the college fund program is that the newly enlisted person contributes $100 per month for the first 12 months.

Once out of the military, some colleges provide credits to veterans based solely on their active duty service. Students should check with the admissions office prior to enrollment.

Tuition Assistance

During active duty, college credits may be earned while enrolled in one of the Army Education Centers through the College Level Exam Program (CLEP), based on job experience or military courses taken while in the service.

The tuition assistance programs offered by the Army, Navy and Air Force *are in addition* to the Montgomery GI Bill and the College Fund. Since many students graduating from high school are undecided about college or what courses to take, the tuition assistance plans are exceptionally attractive for those unsure about career objectives.

Military recruiting programs are subject to change. Students should check with a local recruiter for updates and request all guarantees in writing.

National Guard & Reserve

In addition to the above programs, there are other military options that provide college students with sizable earnings. Students enlisted in the National Guard, the Air National Guard or a military reserve program may earn $300 or more per month while in school.

The Army Reserve will pay back up to $20,000 in student loans whether the participant is a first year student or already graduated. The repayment is 15 percent of the student's loan for each year of service up to $10,000, or for certain specialty positions, 15 percent of the student's loan for each year of service up to $20,000.

The reserve program can be worth $50,000 or more for a commitment of 8 years (6 active reserves; 2 inactive). Requirements include an 8-week basic training camp plus 8 weeks of advanced job training the following summer. All other training camps are 2 weeks in duration. Students receive a military income during the school year for attending a monthly weekend drill.

Once the basic and advanced training is completed, students will also receive the GI Bill every month for 36 months, *plus* earn another $10,000 or more from training camps. In some cases, students may qualify for an enlistment bonus.

For an 8-year commitment in the Air Force Reserve (6 years active; 2 years inactive), the student can share in the Educational Assistance Program. Requirements include a 6-week basic training camp followed by specialized job training for 4 to 52 weeks (from clerk typist to air traffic controller). All other annual camps are 2 weeks.

The Air Force Reserve, National Guard and the Air National Guard will pay students a military income during the school year for attending a monthly weekend drill. Following the basic and advanced training, students will receive the GI Bill every month for 36 months. The commitment is 6 years active service; 2 years inactive. Total remuneration over the 6 years can be $36,000.

In addition to the advanced training, the Air National Guard provides 12 weeks of active duty tech school training prior to college that can be split between 2 summers. The Army National Guard requires 8 weeks of basic training plus advanced training. Depending upon the job specialty, advanced training in both programs can last 4 to 52 weeks. The Reserve and Guard units offer students a monthly stipend guarantee plus competitive wages during training and the 2-week summer camps.

The Air National Guard and the Army National Guard will pay back $10,000 in student or parent loans providing the student is engaged in a specialty career field deemed critical and undermanned. Some states provide full tuition assistance for members of the Air Guard or Army National Guard. Local recruiters can provide details.

Military Academies

Acceptance into a military academy is highly selective. Only 14-15 percent of all applicants are accepted, but the benefits are first-class. The academies offer an outstanding education providing tuition, books, uniforms, room and board and a generous living allowance affording students the opportunity to remain debt free. The normal commitment following graduation is 5 or more years as an active duty officer. Students must apply during the spring of their junior year. The basic admissions requirements include:

- 1900 to 2200 on the SAT
- An exceptionally high math score
- Top 10 to 20 percent of class
- Well rounded in athletics, school, civic or church activities
- A Congressional appointment (except the Coast Guard)

AIR ACADEMY
US Air Force Academy
2304 Cadet Drive Admissions
Colorado Springs, CO 80840-5025
800-443-9266
http://www.academyadmissions.com/

ANNAPOLIS
US Naval Academy
117 Decatur Road
Annapolis, MD 21402-5018
800-638-9156
www.nadn.navy.mil

USMM ACADEMY
US Merchant Marine Academy
Kings Point, New York 11024-1699
800-732-6267
www.usmma.edu

COAST GUARD
US Coast Guard Academy
15 Mohegan Avenue
New London, CT 06320-4195
800-883-8724
www.uscg.mil

WEST POINT
US Military Academy
606 Thayer Road
West Point, NY 10996-1797
800-822-8762
www.usma.edu

Chapter IX

Distance Education

Classes on the Beach?

In some ways, distance learners are unique; they can take classes from anywhere. Many have jobs and families, are highly motivated, and exceptionally determined to graduate.

Those who venture into the world of education at a distance "...must be fairly self-directed and conscientious about completing assignments to succeed in a distance-delivered class," warns Ed Neal, *Phi Kappa Phi Journal*. "Most still require ample and timely feedback on their performance. The demands that distance learning places on the learner make it unlikely that the vast majority of traditional-age college students will be able to succeed under this mode of instruction."

Sustaining

Time is a major factor for anyone who studies online. If you didn't like homework in high school or in a previous college setting, you probably won't like the homework assigned from a distance. It's principally the same. You must do the same type of research, write the same book reports, and pen the same types of papers. The only difference is how the work is sent.

Distance learners normally take tests with an assigned proctor to oversee the process. If you're employed, the proctor may be your supervisor or manager. Often, the virtual school will name an overseer from the local community college. By controlling the testing, the schools involved can maintain standards equal to those of on-campus programs.

Distance professors often employ a mix of written assignments, tests and class participation to assure a fair grade. Many expect participation from online students through videoconferencing. The video portion is normally one-way. An audio portion is 2-way. It allows everyone to ask questions and make statements through a speakerphone. The instructor and other students, including those in the classroom where the live broadcast originates, can all hear and respond.

The term high-tech holds new meaning for those who choose distance education. The minimum requirements include:

- A fax machine

- Color television for video conferencing
- A VCR or DVD recorder
- Voice mail
- A wireless laptop
- High-speed Internet
- A CD-RW-DVD drive
- E-mail for daily assignments

With the expansion of network computing and 2-way video, distance education is rapidly becoming more like a traditional classroom with face-to-face interaction. Many instructors create assignments as team projects to force online students to actively participate with each other via telephone and e-mail and to interact directly with the teacher. Today most colleges deliver coursework via:

- Videocassettes
- DVD's
- E-mail
- Electronic bulletin board
- CD's
- Audio conferencing
- Satellite directed videoconferencing

For some students, there may not be any set meeting time. These students simply download course material from the Internet and discuss the contents via e-mail. For example, the University of Massachusetts Dartmouth Division of Continuing Education delivers courses via e-mail. Courses are structured around a teacher's weekly assignments. Students participate in class through message boards and other electronic means. There is no set time when students must be at their computers. Teachers and students control their own times.

Exploding Growth

When the terms Internet and World Wide Web became household words in the late 1990's, off-campus education received a new lease on life. New terms like distance education, and distance learning appeared. Today most educators believe that distance education is a win-win for both groups involved. Distance learners can save money while getting an education from almost anywhere in the world. The colleges and universities also benefit by increasing their enrollment and tuition income without spending millions on new buildings.

Distance education is not new. Correspondent schools have been part of the educational landscape in the United States for decades. What is new is how educators accept it. You can attend classes from major universities around the country and even receive a bachelor's or master's degree without ever stepping foot on campus. Predictions are that distance learning will graduate 10-15 percent of all students by 2010.

Some say that within the next decade, 25 percent of all graduate courses will be available on the Internet. *"You may have more virtual options than ever before,"* writes Pam Dixon, author of *Virtual College*. "Even stodgy universities that have traditionally snubbed distance education are jumping on the virtual bandwagon."

"With the onslaught of electronic communication, distance education is no longer distant," said Charlotte Thomas, Career and Education Editor at Peterson's. "Technology has irrevocably altered the relationship between student and professor and even what is considered a classroom situation."

Those generating excitement for distance learners include corporate America, government agencies and even military installations. They view distance learning as a way to educate key people without losing them for hours or weeks to on-campus study. As a result, many employers reimburse workers for tuition that leads to a bachelor's or master's degree.

There are very few geographical boundaries today. Note the following examples:

- Georgia Institute of Technology <u>Tech</u> enrolls hundreds in distance education that ends in a Master of Science in Electrical Engineering.
- The University of <u>Phoenix</u> enrolls some 200,000 students around the world, both online as well as at one of their 170 campus sites throughout the country.
- <u>Stanford</u> University offers an online degree in engineering available from every area of the world.
- The online student population of the Graduate School of Management at the University of <u>Dallas</u> represents 50 countries.
- California <u>Virtual</u> University boasts nearly 30,000 students online. Most are working adults with jobs and families. Its Web site includes over 5,000 online courses available from California State Colleges, the University of California, the State's community colleges plus 71 private schools.
- Endicott College in Endicott, Massachusetts, and the University of Maryland University College in College Park, Maryland, offer online degrees and give students the opportunity to earn legitimate college credits based on work and life experience. See <u>Credit for Life</u>. When a student completes an academic career assessment, the university gives him or her recommended study programs and the opportunity to select from thousands of available courses. Students enrolled at Endicott College may petition for up to

30 proficiency credits for work and life experience. Students without any previous college history can take entry-level courses and earn their degree through EC Online at <u>Endicott</u>.)

- University of Maryland University College <u>UMUC</u> has a cooperative education program and offers up to 15 upper-level course credits toward a bachelor's degree.

- The University of Maryland University College offered its first distance education courses in 1972. Today its highly successful Bachelor's Degree at a Distance enrolls students from around the world. Through their EXCELL program, distance learners may apply for up to 30 academic credits toward their undergraduate degree in one of 2 ways:

1. Credit for previous work and life experience

2. College credit by examination

NOTE: *Be especially wary of the scam operators who sell fake diplomas based on work experience. Many of the names sound authentic, but are really bogus diploma mills claiming to be accredited, often using phony accreditation names.*

Some educators argue that distance learning is more stimulating and encourage more critical reasoning than traditional large lecture classes because of the interaction that takes place in small-group settings. According to Jerald G. Schutte, California State University, Northridge, <u>CalState</u>, test scores for both mid-term and final examinations were on average 20 percent higher for online students vs. those students in a traditional classroom.

A study published by <u>eCollege</u>, noted that 85 percent of the faculty respondents said their students learned equally effectively online as on campus, and some did even better.

Hundreds of students are enrolled in America's first fully accredited virtual institution, Jones International University. JIU has no campus, no pretty buildings and no student union. Instead, the school delivers a virtual classroom electronically to participants wherever they live via the Internet. For more information on earning a bachelor's or master's degree online, call 888-811-5663 or log on Jones International.

Another method for awarding certificates and degrees was developed by the planning board for Western Governors University. The Governors of eighteen western states and one US territory founded the virtual institution with a vision of making higher education more accessible. Thousands of courses are available through WGU from hundreds of participating schools. Based on knowledge of a particular subject, a student can earn a degree or certificate by demonstrating a superior grasp of that subject through a WGU assessment. Instead of being credit-based, Western Governors University is a competency-based institution. More information may be found at Western Governors.

In *Distance Degrees,* Mark Wilson notes that both accredited Excelsior College and Thomas Edison State College in New Jersey (Edison) will grant a Bachelor's degree based solely on credits earned from passing equivalency examinations and/or from life experience.

Other notable accredited schools online include:
Auburn University (www.auburn.edu)
Colorado State University (www.colostate.edu)
Columbia University (www.cvn.columbia.edu)
Duke University (www.fuqua.duke.edu)
Golden State University (cybercampus.ggu.edu/)
Iowa State University (www.iastate.edu)
Stephens College (www.stephens.edu)
Syracuse University (www.suce.syr.edu)

> U of Arizona, (www.asu.edu)
> U of Colorado, Boulder (www.colorado.edu)
> U of Massachusetts, Amherst www.umass.edu
> Washington State University (www.eus.wsu.edu)

Students who apply for admission into one of the hundreds of virtual or distance learning institutions will find it no different from applying for admittance to a traditional college or university.

Applications, essays, and SAT®/ACT® scores will still be required for those without any prior college history. For those going back to college online, a transcript from a previous college must be sent to the online school. Those seeking an advanced graduate degree are usually required to take the Graduate Record Exam (GRE) or the Graduate Management Admission Test (GMAT) prior to admittance.

Online Success

Dr. Debra Mertz at www.worldwidelearn.com is an online graduate and offers tips on how to succeed in getting your degree online:

10 Tips for Success in Online Learning (Dr. Debra Mertz)

1. Be flexible and open to new learning. While online classes involve more effort than on ground classes because they are usually accelerated courses/programs, be sure to follow directions, they are there to aid you. Utilize the resources available to you. You have the instructor, your classmates, the online library, the Internet, organizations and more.

2. Have patience with yourself and others. Don't be so hard on yourself. Allow yourself time to adjust to the new environment. It will not happen overnight, but give it a chance.

Frustration builds all too quickly. Take it slow, one step at a time. Set aside priority time for yourself to study.

3. Ask questions as needed. Clarify all expectations upfront. There are no dumb questions, other than the one(s) not asked.

4. Watch all deadlines. Do not blame the instructor when it is your responsibility as a student to adhere to timeframes. If the unexpected happens, contact your instructor immediately-they are people and will understand things happen in life. Often times, this is overlooked.

5. Check and double-check all of your work before submitting it, especially for a grade. This includes grammar, punctuation & spelling.

6. Respect your instructor and classmates. They are people with real feelings, even if you can't see them because they are online.

7. Actively participate. Be active in the classroom. Share your experiences and knowledge in the classroom. Back up your experience and knowledge with real data-this builds substance. This is where learning takes place. Participation is usually a very big item in online classes since this is where discussions build more learning and new knowledge.

8. Have patience. Issues will arise. Expect the unexpected, especially with technology. Keep the tech support number handy at all times.

9. Take time to read and comprehend all materials. Most students err here as they do not allocate enough time for reading and/ or comprehension of materials and find themselves missing critical data/instructions.

10. Take the online classroom environment seriously, while

having FUN. While grades are important, it is not the major reason to take a class. Learning is fundamental and is the sole responsibility of the student, not the instructor. If you do not put in an "A" effort, do not expect an "A". If you only do mediocre work, accept it, and do not blame your instructor.

Evaluating Online Schools

Before filling out an application online, students need to ask direct questions: "Is the school fully accredited, and if so, by whose authority?" "What is the cost per credit unit?" "How does this compare to the costs at traditional schools for the same program?" "How long does it take to complete each course or program?" "How is the coursework delivered?" "Does the school accept transfer credits from other distance learning institutions?" "Do the programs meet the Federal Government's guidelines for student financial aid?"

Other questions might include: "What percent of the faculty hold a Master's degree or Doctorate? Do the professors have regular office hours for teacher-student phone conferences? Are textbooks purchased online or locally? Does the school provide software training prior to any course delivery?"

As more institutions are accredited, students are discovering the multiplicity of courses and degrees available online. It is critical however, that the institutions have been accredited by either the federal government or the Council for Higher Education Accreditation CHEA.

"Don't get pulled in by one of those sham operators," warns Mark Wilson "There are illegal schools that essentially sell worthless paper [degrees]." For a list of accredited online education providers, check out Distant Ed from the American Educational Guidance Center. For a complete listing of the regional accreditation agencies including the states they represent see Accreditation.

The US Department of Education also recognizes the Distance Education & Training Council (DETC) which publishes a list of schools they endorse nationwide.

Some of the institutions accredited by DETC include schools that offer courses on interior design at www.rhodec.com. Other students may venture out and study to be a Graduate Gemologist at www.gia. edu, earn a Bachelor of Science in Health Services/Management at www.cchs.edu, or an Associate's Degree in criminal justice at Andrew Jackson. For a complete listing, call the Distance Education & Training Council at 202- 234-5100.

As distance education continues to grow, students are also able to earn their Bachelor's or Master's Degree online at Moody or Liberty. For an updated list of schools offering online degrees, log onto ClassesUSA.

Chapter X

Student Loans

(THE LAST RESORT)

Federal Stafford Loan

Depending on your Expected Family Contribution (EFC), you can borrow up to $65,000 in subsidized Stafford Loans, and another $73,000 in unsubsidized loans. If your loan is subsidized, the government pays the interest while you're in school and during the 6-month grace period after graduation. If the loan is unsubsidized, the interest must either be paid quarterly or accrue and be added to the total cost of your loan at graduation.

As a dependent undergraduate student, you may borrow $2,600 as a freshman, $3,500 as a sophomore and $5,500 per year thereafter up to $20,000. You don't need assets or credit. You can borrow the money regardless of past credit problems. Moreover, if your parents are unable to qualify for a parent loan, you can borrow an additional $23,000 in unsubsidized funds.

WARNING: Borrowing Stafford loan money with a maximum interest rate of 8.25 percent can become your worst nightmare after graduation and launch you into years of financial bondage.

The following example is for a *subsidized* Stafford Loan. Should the loan be unsubsidized, the total cost and payments would be even *greater*.

	TOTAL INTEREST & FEES FOR *SUBSIDIZED* STAFFORD LOAN INCLUDING ORIGINATION FEES				
Plan	Loan	Interest*	Mo. Pmts.	Actual Payback	Percentile ‡
10 yr.	$10,000	6.80 %	$115	$14,200	42 %
15 yr.	$10,000	6.80 %	$ 89	$16,420	64 %
20 yr.	$10,000	6.80 %	$ 76	$18,640	86 %
10 yr.	$15,000	6.80 %	$173	$21,360	42 %
15 yr.	$15,000	6.80 %	$134	$24,720	64 %
20 yr.	$15,000	6.80 %	$114	$27,960	86 %

* Rates change every July 1st. Maximum rate is 8.25 percent plus origination fee.
‡Payback and percentile figures are rounded and include 4 percent origination fee.

Stafford Loans have a 2 to 4 percent origination fee. A typical $10,000 loan can cost $400 just for the privilege of borrowing, which is in addition to the finance charge. If the 4 percent origination fee was added to the maximum allowable interest of 8.25 percent, you could end up paying **more than double** the amount borrowed. Until Uncle Sam eliminates the 3 to 4 percent origination fee, the Stafford Loan can never be considered a "low-cost" student loan. Once they see the real **cost** of student loans, many students sensibly reject them.

To add to the confusion of the situation, both the Stafford and the Parent Loan for Undergraduate Students (PLUS) have 2 variations. Under the direct loan program, the money is disbursed directly from the federal government. Under the Federal Family Education Loan Program (FFELP), the money is borrowed from a third-party lender with interest rates set by the government. The colleges and universities choose the type of loan program they offer their students.

"Student loans themselves are not the problem," said the late Larry Burkett, co-founder of Crown Financial Ministries. "The problem is that students often borrow in excess of what they need to get a college education. A student loan should only be considered the 'last resort.'"

Rating Financial Aid Packages

Colleges mail their award letters or financial aid packages in the spring and summer. Many parents and students are shocked to see the financial aid packages bursting with Stafford Loans. If you receive an award letter that is unacceptable, make an appointment with the *head* of the financial aid department. Having a face-to-face meeting accomplishes two things: 1) it allows you and your parents an opportunity to begin building a relationship with the Financial Aid Administrator, and 2) it allows parents a platform to discuss any unusual expenses not noted on the financial aid form. An administrator cannot arbitrarily change your EFC. Based on unusual circumstances, the administrator may adjust the components that determine your overall contribution at his or her discretion,.

Since the amount of non-repayable grants versus repayable loans differs widely from school to school, many parents and students shop colleges for the best financial aid. If one school offers a better aid package than another, the competing school may make a more favorable counter offer. Some colleges, especially private schools, are very competitive and will negotiate. Other schools will not and may be offended at the suggestion.

Forbearance & Deferment

With the accelerated increase in student loans, the government has added a repayment clause allowing students to receive forbearance up to 3 years if the student loan debt is greater than 20 percent of their income. Under forbearance, students can make smaller loan payments for a designated period of time.

Under special conditions, some students may be eligible for loan deferment. The loan payments may be deferred if:

- The borrower is pursuing at least a half time course of study
- The borrower is enrolled in a graduate fellowship program
- The borrower is disabled and in rehabilitation training.

Details for forbearance and deferment are available from the college financial aid office or by clicking onto Loan Deferment.

Teacher Forgiveness

The revised Teacher Forgiveness Program allows up to $17,500 of a student's expensive Stafford Loan to be cancelled. To be eligible, a borrower must first work as a full-time teacher for 5 consecutive years teaching math, science, special education, or working in low income or teacher shortage areas. During the 5-year period, the borrower is expected to repay his or her subsidized or unsubsidized loans in a normal manner. At the end of 5 years, the government will cancel up to $17,500 of the remaining balance. See details at Loan Forgiveness. To determine if your teaching assignment falls within a teacher shortage area, see Teachers.

Federal Plus Loan

The Parent Loan for Undergraduate Students (PLUS) is set up exactly like the Stafford Loan with either the U.S. Department of Education disbursing funds through the school to the parents, or third-party lenders disbursing funds under the Federal Family Education Loan Program (FFELP). Under the direct program, borrowers have a choice of 3 different repayment plans. The standard parent loan is still funded by banks, credit unions, and insurance companies. Repayment begins within 60 days of the loan origination unless the lender agrees to a deferment. The standard repayment plan requires a minimum of $50 per month up to 10 years. The extended plan also has a minimum of

$50 per month but continues up to 30 years. The graduated repayment plan allows for reduced payments followed by arbitrary increases every 24 months for 30 years. Parents are permitted to borrow an unlimited amount under the PLUS program, not to exceed the cost of education.

The interest on the Parent Loan is considerably higher than the Stafford Loan. The PLUS is based on the 52-week T-Bill, plus 3.1 percent adjusted annually, not to exceed 9 percent.

Ed Note: Like the Stafford Loan, there is a 3 to 4 percent loan fee deducted from each disbursement making the PLUS an outrageous funding alternative.

The PLUS Loan is not service-cancelable and may only be discharged for permanent and total disability, or if the student, for whom the parent borrowed the loan, should die.

Federal Perkins Loan

The Federal Perkins Loan is one of the most sought-after financial aid programs available. The loan is need-based, funded by the government, and administered by the colleges. Undergraduate students may borrow up to $4,000 per year to a maximum of $20,000. Graduate students may borrow an additional $20,000. Best of all, the government pays the interest while the student is in school.

10 yrs	$ 5,000	5%	$ 53	$ 1,364	$ 6,364	27.3%
10 yrs	$10,000	5%	$106	$ 2,728	$12,728	27.3%
10 yrs	$15,000	5%	$159	$ 4,092	$19.092	27.3%
10 yrs	$20,000	5%	$212	$ 5,457	$25,457	27.3%
10 yrs	$40,000	5%	$424	$10,914	$50,914	27.3%

What makes the Perkins Loan so popular is the 5 percent flat interest rate compared to an adjustable rate that can go as high as 8.25 percent for the Stafford Loan and 9 percent for the Parent Loan. Based on the figures above, the monthly payment for a $5,000 Perkins Loan is only $53. The interest is $1,364 with a total payback $6,364, or 27.3 percent of the original loan amount.

The Perkins Loan has a 9-month grace period after graduation, and allows the student up to 10 years to complete the loan repayment. Furthermore, there is no loan origination fee, which saves the student an additional 3 to 4 percent.

The Perkins Loan is service-cancelable under the following conditions: (See Loan Forgiveness)

One hundred percent of the Federal Perkins Loan, including interest, may be canceled if the borrower is a full-time teacher in a math, science, foreign languages, bilingual education, special education, any other field of expertise where the state agency determines a shortage, or in a school system serving low-income students. For a complete listing of all teacher shortage areas within the U.S., log on Teachers.

One hundred percent of the Federal Perkins Loan may be forgiven if the borrower is a full-time practical or registered nurse, or a licensed medical technician providing health care services.

One hundred percent is cancelable if the borrower is a full-time employee at a public or private nonprofit child or family service agency providing services for 1) high-risk children at risk of abuse and neglect or 2) children who have serious emotional, mental or behavioral disturbances.

One hundred percent of the Perkins Loan is service-cancelable if a borrower is a full-time qualified professional provider of early intervention services. One hundred percent of a student's Perkins loan is service-cancelable if the borrower is a full-time law enforcement or corrections officer at the local, state or federal level. In today's environment, that could mean working in counter-terrorism, forensics, as a CSI investigator, or airport security.

CANCELLATION RATE: 15 percent first and second year

20 percent third and fourth year

30 percent fifth year

If the borrower is a full-time staff member in the educational part of a Head Start preschool program, up to 70 percent of the student loan may be cancelled at the rate of 15 percent per year for each year of employment.

To determine eligibility, the student must apply for cancellation by filing the required forms at the school where the loan originated. School officials determine whether the student is entitled to have any portion of the loan canceled.

Like the Stafford Loan, the Federal Perkins Loan may be canceled for death or permanent and total disability.

Other Service-Cancelable Loans

There are other loans that can be erased with service. Students with exceptional need studying medicine, pharmacy, osteopathy, dentistry, optometry, or veterinary medicine may be eligible for the government's Health Professional Student Loan. The program covers tuition plus $2,500 per year. The interest on the loan does not accrue while the student attends classes or completes a residency.

The loan may be canceled in the event of death or total disability or under the following conditions: Up to 85 percent of the student loan is service-cancelable if the borrower practices in a shortage area as determined by the government. The program allows for 60 percent of the loan to be forgiven during the first 2 years of service and another 25 percent if the participant remains for a third year in the same area. Most medical school administrators have details on the program.

Still another opportunity for professional students is the National

Health Service Corps Scholarship. The program is a service obligation scholarship designed for Osteopaths seeking a Master's degree, students in medical school or a Physician's Assistant program, or Registered Nurses studying to be Nurse Practitioners and/or Certified Nurse Midwives.

The scholarship covers all tuition and fees plus an additional $800 per month for living expenses. The obligation is canceled upon death, permanent and total disability or under the following conditions:

Participants must agree to work full-time for a period of 2 years at a public hospital, a rural health clinic, or a health facility with a critical shortage of nurses. Government programs change frequently. Interested students should check out National Health Service Corps, or call 800-638-0824.

The National Health Service Corps Loan Repayment Program from the U.S. Department of Health & Human Services is available for students in certain healthcare fields. Eligible candidates include students who have completed at least one year of medical school or training including medical doctors or Osteopathic physicians with specialties in family medicine, general pediatrics, internal medicine, general psychiatry, OB/GYN, Physician's Assistants, Nurse Practitioners, Nurse Midwives, Dentists, Dental Hygienists, Clinical Psychologists, clinical social workers, psychiatric nurse specialists, or marriage and family therapists.

The U.S. Department of Health & Human Services offers participants repayment of qualified loans if they serve for a period of 2 years in a medically underserved community as determined by the Department. Participants are offered a competitive salary plus the repayment of $25,000 in student loans each year for 2 years. Candidates may request an extension of 2 additional years for a repayment of up to $35,000 per year thereafter, plus a stipend equal to 39 percent of the loan to compensate for additional taxes. Total value: $120,000 plus tax stipend. For up-to-date information, contact NHSC Loan Repayment Program online at Loan Repayment, or write 2070 Chain Bridge Road, Suite 450, Vienna, Virginia 22182, 800-221-9393.

MedSend Program

Healthcare professionals who prefer to avoid government programs may wish to contact Project MedSend. This unique program is specifically designed to repay student loans owed by healthcare professionals while they serve as medical missionaries in medically underserved areas.

Applicants must first be called to use their medical training for the spread of the Gospel, be under the authority of a recognized Christian mission organization and be within 18 months of leaving for a career as a medical missionary. Applicants must also show fiscal responsibility and stewardship maturity, demonstrate a missionary lifestyle, and be in the process of paying off their student loans while serving as an Intern or in residency. In addition to the Student Loan Repayment Grant, Project MedSend also offers financial counseling to healthcare professionals concerning student borrowing. For more information, write Project MedSend at P.O. Box 1098, Orange, Connecticut 06470-7098, or call 203-891-8223 or online at MedSend.

AVOIDING STUDENT LOAN DEBT

NOTE: ALL INTERNET LINKS IN *TheCollegeTrap* ARE UNDERLINED.
TO ACTIVATE THE WEB LINKS, GO TO WWW.THECOLLEGETRAP.INFO

STUDENT LOAN TRAP

"Avoid the student loan trap," notes author at Bankrate.com.
Columnist, Lucy Lazarony, highlights a program where students
compare financial aid packages received from 3 different schools with
the help of an online cost calculator.

STUDENT ABUSE?

Students need to carefully consider the cost of any student loan offer.
One student received a brochure offering her $25,000 for her graduate
studies. The payback was $267 per month for 20 years, or a total of
$64,171. The lender also acknowledged a loan of $120,000 at $1,262
per month for 20 years. That works out to be over $300,000, or 152.5
percent interest.

STUDENT LOAN REPAYMENT

If your loan is in default or nearing default, or if you simply want more
information about repaying your student loan, check out the online
brochure from the office of Student Assistance. For information on
deferments and forbearance, see Loan Deferment.

LOW COST STAFFORD LOAN?

The interest rate on adjustable rate loans changes every year. Don't
forget the 3 to 4 percent origination fee added on top of the current
rate and deducted from each disbursement of funds. Until the
Government eliminates the origination fees, the Stafford Loan can
never be considered a "low-cost" student loan.

INCREDIBLE LOAN PAYBACK PROGRAM

The Office of Personnel Management (OPM) in Washington reports an increase in the number of students taking advantage of their student loan payback. Basically the program is used to recruit or retain highly qualified personnel for government agencies. Each agency is authorized under 5 U.S.C. 5379 to offer the program to qualified employees, whether graduated or not. The agencies are allowed to pay back $10,000 in student loans per year up to a maximum of $60,000. What's the catch? First of all there is no guarantee that you will automatically qualify for the program. The loan payback program is part of the up-front employment recruiting process that you negotiate. Secondly, you must remain with the government for a minimum of 3 years. If you leave ahead of that, you're required to reimburse OPM for the total amount of the loan payback. Thirdly, the payback is taxable and the $10,000 will be taxed as ordinary income. Make sure you get everything in writing. For more information, click on Questions & Answers.

Appendix One

Tax Credits

Hope Credit

The Hope Credit is a Federal program that allows a tax credit of $1,500 per year for qualified education expenses for the first 2 years, providing the student is pursuing an undergraduate degree or recognized education credential. You may be eligible for a tax credit equal to 100 percent of the first $1,000 of tuition and 50 percent of the second $1,000 of tuition for your freshman and sophomore years.

The Hope credit is a nonrefundable credit. This means that it can reduce your tax to zero, but if the credit is more than your tax, the excess will not be refunded. Income limitations are subject to an AGI of no more than $52,000 for a single person or $105,000 for joint filers.

If you're eligible to claim the Hope credit and the lifetime learning credit for the same student in the same year, you can choose to claim either of the 2 credits, but not both. If you pay qualified education expenses for more than one student in the same year, you can claim the Hope credit for one student and the lifetime learning credit for another student in the same year.

Lifetime Learning Credit

You may be able to claim a Lifetime Learning Credit of up to $2,000 for qualified education expenses paid for all students enrolled in eligible educational institutions. There is no limit on the number of years the lifetime learning credit can be claimed for each student.

The Lifetime Learning Credit works the same as the Hope Credit, i.e., if the credit is more than your tax the excess will not be refunded. The income limitations are the same as the Hope Credit.

Student Loan Interest Deduction

If your modified adjusted gross income is less than $65,000 ($130,000 if filing a joint return), there is a special deduction allowed for those paying interest on a student loan used for higher education. The deduction is claimed as an adjustment to income so you do not need to itemize your deductions on Form 1040. This deduction can reduce the amount of your income subject to tax by up to $2,500. More information on student loan interest deduction and other education benefits is available in Publication 970, *Tax Benefits for Education.*

Employer Provided Education Assistance

If you receive educational assistance benefits from your employer under an educational assistance program, you can exclude up to $5,250 of those benefits each year. This means your employer should not include the benefits with your wages, tips, and other compensation shown in box 1 of your Form W-2. This also means that you do not have to include the benefits on your income tax return. You cannot use any of the tax-free education expenses paid for by your employer as the basis for any other deduction or credit, including the Federal Hope Credit and the Lifetime Learning Credit.

HELPFUL WEB LINKS

NOTE: ALL INTERNET LINKS IN *TheCollegeTrap* ARE UNDERLINED.
TO ACTIVATE THE WEB LINKS, GO TO WWW.THECOLLEGETRAP.INFO

529 INVESTMENT FUNDS

A 529 Plan may be a family's best investment tool to offset the
increasing cost of college, especially for parents with children in
elementary or middle schools. It is also a great place for parents or
grandparents to add to a student's college savings account without
the usual tax consequences. For more information, see Chapter VI
or 529 Plans, Comparative Plans, Enterprise, College Savings and
Vanguard.

RED FLAG ON IRAs AND 529s

Here's a story regarding the misuse of IRAs and 529 plans when
purchasing equipment and materials for college students. Before you
buy, read IRAs vs. IRS.

Appendix Two
Sample Budget

(Based on $19,615 estimate including tuition, room & board, travel, etc.)

SUGGESTED MONTHLY SPENDING PLAN CATEGORIES

TAF *(TOTAL AVAILABLE FUNDS)*: $ 2180

Salary or tips if employed	$ 280	
Savings or Checking	$ 100	
Parent's	$ 1000	
Loans & Scholarships	$ 800	
Other	$	

T&T *(LESS TAXES & TITHE)*: $ 218
NSI *(NET SPENDABLE INCOME)*: $ 1962

LESS MONTHLY EXPENSES:

Housing Costs $ 354

Rent/Mortgage	$ 211
Utilities	$ 76
Telephone	$ 67

(Divide totals by number of roommates)

Food Allowance $ 295
Tuition & Fees $ 438
Books $ 86

(Divide annual totals by 9 months)

Transportation Expenses $ 371

Car Payments	$ 270
Car Insurance	*Dad*
Gas & Oil	$ 66
Car Repairs	$ 35

Clothing Allowance $ 36
Entertainment $ 80

Restaurants	$ 30
Movie Rentals	$ 12
Social Events	$ 38

LESS MONTHLY EXPENSES (cont.):

Medical Allowance			$	*40*
	Doctor	$ *Ins*		
	Dentist	$ *Dad*		
	Prescriptions	$ *10*		
	Other	$		
Debts			$	*45*
	Credit Cards	$		
	Loans	$		
	Revolving	$ *45*		
	Other	$		
Insurance (other than car)			$	
Savings (Bank/Mutual Funds, etc.)			$	*20*
Miscellaneous			$	*197*
	Gifts	$ *12*		
	Cosmetics/Shaving	$ *26*		
	Haircuts/Perms	$ *28*		
	Laundry	$ *18*		
	Cleaning Supplies	$ *18*		
	Fraternity/Sorority Dues	$ *50*		
	Music Supplies	$ *10*		
	Art Supplies	$		
	Extra Date Money	$ *25*		
	Other	$ *10*		
	Other	$		
Child Care (If Applicable)			$	

TOTAL EXPENSES	$	*1962*
DIFFERENCE PER MONTH	$	*0*

Note: if the expenses equal more than income or revenues, reduce your expenses until there is a zero balance at the end of each month.

Budget Worksheets

MONTHLY SPENDING PLAN CATEGORIES

TAF *(TOTAL AVAILABLE FUNDS):* $ _____

Salary or tips if employed $ _____

Savings or Checking $ _____

Parent's $ _____

Loans & Scholarships $ _____

Other $ _____

T&T *(LESS TAXES & TITHE):* $ _____

NSI *(NET SPENDABLE INCOME):* $ _____

LESS MONTHLY EXPENSES:

Housing Costs $ _____

      Rent/Mortgage $ _____

      Utilities $ _____

      Telephone $ _____

      (Divide totals by number of roommates)

Food Allowance $ _____

Tuition & Fees $ _____

Books $ _____

      (Divide annual totals by 9 months)

Transportation Expenses $ _____

      Car Payments $ _____

      Car Insurance $ _____

      Gas & Oil $ _____

      Car Repairs $ _____

Clothing Allowance $ _____

Entertainment $ _____

      Restaurants $ _____

      Movie Rentals $ _____

      Social Events $ _____

LESS MONTHLY EXPENSES (cont.):

Medical Allowance $ _____

      Doctor $ _____

      Dentist $ _____

      Prescriptions $ _____

      Other $ _____

Debts $ _____

      Credit Cards $ _____

      Loans $ _____

      Revolving $ _____

      Other $ _____

Insurance (other than car) $ _____

Savings (Bank/Mutual Funds, etc.) $ _____

Miscellaneous $ _____

      Gifts $ _____

      Cosmetics/Shaving $ _____

      Haircuts/Perms $ _____

      Laundry $ _____

      Cleaning Supplies $ _____

      Fraternity/Sorority Dues $ _____

      Music Supplies $ _____

      Art Supplies $ _____

      Extra Date Money $ _____

      Other $ _____

      Other $ _____

Child Care (If Applicable) $ _____

TOTAL EXPENSES $ _____

DIFFERENCE PER MONTH $ _____

Note: if the expenses equal more than income or revenues, reduce your expenses until there is a zero balance at the end of each month.

Budget Worksheets

MONTHLY SPENDING PLAN CATEGORIES

TAF *(TOTAL AVAILABLE FUNDS)*: $ _____

Salary or tips if employed $ _____

Savings or Checking $ _____

Parent's $ _____

Loans & Scholarships $ _____

Other $ _____

T&T *(LESS TAXES & TITHE)*: $ _____

NSI *(NET SPENDABLE INCOME)*: $ _____

LESS MONTHLY EXPENSES:

Housing Costs $ _____

    Rent/Mortgage $ _____

    Utilities $ _____

    Telephone $ _____

    (Divide totals by number of roommates)

Food Allowance $ _____

Tuition & Fees $ _____

Books $ _____

    (Divide annual totals by 9 months)

Transportation Expenses $ _____

    Car Payments $ _____

    Car Insurance $ _____

    Gas & Oil $ _____

    Car Repairs $ _____

Clothing Allowance $ _____

Entertainment $ _____

    Restaurants $ _____

    Movie Rentals $ _____

    Social Events $ _____

LESS MONTHLY EXPENSES (cont.):

Medical Allowance $ _____

        Doctor $ _____

        Dentist $ _____

        Prescriptions $ _____

        Other $ _____

Debts $ _____

        Credit Cards $ _____

        Loans $ _____

        Revolving $ _____

        Other $ _____

Insurance (other than car) $ _____

Savings (Bank/Mutual Funds, etc.) $ _____

Miscellaneous $ _____

        Gifts $ _____

        Cosmetics/Shaving $ _____

        Haircuts/Perms $ _____

        Laundry $ _____

        Cleaning Supplies $ _____

        Fraternity/Sorority Dues $ _____

        Music Supplies $ _____

        Art Supplies $ _____

        Extra Date Money $ _____

        Other $ _____

        Other $ _____

Child Care (If Applicable) $ _____

TOTAL EXPENSES $ _____

DIFFERENCE PER MONTH $ _____

Note: if the expenses equal more than income or revenues, reduce your expenses until there is a zero balance at the end of each month.

Appendix Three

State Grant Agencies

Alabama
Alabama Commission on Higher Education
P.O. Box 302000
Montgomery, AL 36130-2000
Phone: (334) 242-1998
Toll-Free: (800) 960-7773
Toll-Free Restrictions: AL residents only
Fax: (334) 242-0268
Website: http://www.ache.state.al.us/

Alaska
Alaska Commission on Postsecondary
Education
3030 Vintage Boulevard
Juneau, AK 99801-7100
Phone: (907) 465-2962
Toll-Free: (800) 441-2962
Fax: (907) 465-5316
TTY: (907) 465-3143
Email: customer_service@acpe.state.ak.us
Website: http://alaskadvantage.state.ak.us/

Arizona
Arizona Commission for Postsecondary
Education
2020 North Central Avenue, Suite 550
Phoenix, AZ 85004-4503
Phone: (602) 258-2435
Fax: (602) 258-2483
Website: http://www.azhighered.org/

Arkansas
Arkansas Department of Higher
Education
114 East Capitol
Little Rock, AR 72201-3818
Phone: (501) 371-2000
Fax: (501) 371-2001
Website: http://www.arkansashighered.
com/

California
California Student Aid
Commission
P.O. Box 419027
Rancho Cordova, CA 95741-9027
Phone: (916) 526-7590
Fax: (916) 526-8004
Email: custsvcs@csac.ca.gov or
studentsupport@csac.ca.gov
Website: http://www.csac.ca.gov/

Colorado
Colorado Commission on Higher
Education
1380 Lawrence Street, Suite 1200
Denver, CO 80204
Phone: (303) 866-2723
Fax: (303) 866-4266
Email: CCHE@state.co.us
Website: http://www.state.co.us/cche/

Connecticut
Connecticut Department of Higher
Education
61 Woodland Street
Hartford, CT 06105-2326
Toll-Free: (800) 842-0229
Fax: (860) 947-1310
Email: info@ctdhe.org
Website: http://www.ctdhe.org/

Delaware
Delaware Higher Education Commission
820 North French Street
Wilmington, DE 19801
Toll-Free: (800) 292-7935
Fax: (302) 577-6765
Email: dhec@state.de.us
Website: http://www.doe.state.de.us/
high-ed/

District of Columbia
State Education Office (District of
Columbia)
Suite 350 North,
441 Fourth Street, NW
Washington, DC 20001
Phone: (202) 727-2824
Toll-Free: (877) 485-6751
Fax: (202) 727-2834
Email: seo@dc.gov
http://seo.dc.gov/main.shtm

Georgia
Georgia Student Finance Commission
State Loans Division
Suite 230
2082 East Exchange Place
Tucker, GA 30084
Phone: (770) 724-9000
Toll-Free: (800) 505-4732
Fax: (770) 724-9089
Email: info@gsfc.org
Website: http://www.gsfc.org/

Hawaii
Hawaii State Postsecondary Education
Commission
Room 209, 2444 Dole Street
Honolulu, HI 96822-2302
Phone: (808) 956-8213
Fax: (808) 956-5156

Idaho
Idaho State Board of Education
P.O. Box 83720
Boise, ID 83720-0037
Phone: (208) 334-2270
Fax: (208) 334-2632
Email: board@osbe.idaho.gov
Website: http://www.boardofed.idaho.
gov/

Illinois
Illinois Student Assistance Commission
1755 Lake Cook Road
Deerfield, IL 60015-5209
Phone: (847) 948-8500
Toll-Free: (800) 899-4722
Fax: (847) 831-8549
TTY: (847) 831-8326
Email: collegezone@isac.org
Website: http://www.collegezone.com/

Indiana
State Student Assistance
150 West Market Street
Indianapolis, IN 46204-2811
Phone: (317) 232-2350
Toll-Free: (888) 528-4719
Toll-Free Restrictions: IN residents only
Fax: (317) 232-3260
Email: grants@ssaci.state.in.us
Website: http://www.ssaci.in.gov/

Iowa
Student Aid Commission
Fourth Floor, 200 10th Street
Des Moines, IA 50309
Phone: (515) 242-3344
Toll-Free. (800) 383-4222
Fax: (515) 242-3388
Email: info@iowacollegeaid.org
Website: http://www.iowacollegeaid.org/

Kansas
Kansas Board of Regents
Curtis State Office Building
Suite 520
1000 SW Jackson Street
Topeka, KS 66612-1368
Phone: (785) 296-3421
Fax: (785) 296-0983
Website: http://www.kansasregents.org/

Kentucky
Higher Education Authority
P.O. Box 798
Frankfort, KY 40602-0798
Phone: (502) 696-7200
Toll-Free: (800) 928-8926
Fax: (502) 696-7496
Email: inquiries@kheaa.com
Website: http://www.kheaa.com/

Louisiana
Louisiana Office of Student Financial
Assistance
P.O. Box 91202
Baton Rouge, LA 70821-9202
Phone: (225) 922-1012
Toll-Free: (800) 259-5626
Fax: (225) 922-0790
Email: custserv@osfa.state.la.us
Website: http://www.osfa.state.la.us/

Maine
Finance Authority of Maine
P.O. Box 949
Augusta, ME 04332-0949
Phone: (207) 623-3263 x313
Fax: (207) 623-0095
TTY: (207) 626-2717
Email: info@famemaine.com
Website: http://www.famemaine.com/

Maryland
Maryland Higher Education
Commission
Suite 400
839 Bestgate Road
Annapolis, MD 21401-3013
Phone: (410) 260-4500
Toll-Free: (800) 974-1024
Fax: (410) 974-5994
Website: http://www.mhec.state.md.us/

Massachusetts
Massachusetts Board of Higher
Education
Room 1401, One Ashburton Place
Boston, MA 02108-1696
Phone: (617) 994-6950
Fax: (617) 727-6397
Website: http://www.mass.edu/

Massachusetts
Massachusetts Higher Education
Boston Public Library
700 Boylston Street
Boston, MA 02116
Phone: (617) 536-0200
Toll-Free: (877) 332-4348
Fax: (617) 536-4737
Website: http://www.edinfo.org/

Michigan
Higher Education Assistance
Office of Scholarships and Grants
P.O. Box 30462
Lansing, MI 48909-7962
Phone: (517) 373-3394
Toll-Free: (888) 447-2687
Fax: (517) 241-5835
Email: osg@michigan.gov
Website: www.michigan.gov/mistudentaid/

Minnesota
Office of Higher Education
Suite 350
1450 Energy Park Drive
Saint Paul, MN 55108-5227
Phone: (651) 642-0567
Toll-Free: (800) 657-3866
Fax: (651) 642-0675
Email: info@heso.state.mn.us
Website: http://www.ohe.state.mn.us/

Mississippi
Mississippi Office of Student Financial Aid
3825 Ridgewood Road
Jackson, MS 39211-6453
 Toll-Free: (800) 327-2980
Fax: (601) 432-6527
Email: sfa@ihl.state.ms.us
www.mississippiuniversities.com/

Missouri
Missouri Department of Higher Education
3515 Amazonas Drive
Jefferson City, MO 65109
Phone: (573) 751-2361
Toll-Free: (800) 473-6757
Fax: (573) 751-6635
TTY: (800) 735-2966
Email: info@dhe.mo.gov
Website: http://www.dhe.mo.gov/

Montana
Montana University System
2500 Broadway
Helena, MT 59620-3101
Phone: (406) 444-6570
Fax: (406) 444-1469
Website: http://www.montana.edu/wwwoche/

Nebraska
Nebraska Coordinating Commission
for Postsecondary Education
Suite 300, 140 North Eighth Street
P.O. Box 95005
Lincoln, NE 68509-5005
Phone: (402) 471-2847
Fax: (402) 471-2886
Website: http://www.ccpe.state.ne.us/PublicDoc/CCPE/Default.asp

New Hampshire
New Hampshire Postsecondary
Education Commission
3 Barrell Court
Concord, NH 03301-8543
Phone: (603) 271-2555
Fax: (603) 271-2696
TTY: (800) 735-2964
www.state.nh.us/ postsecondary

New Jersey
Commission on Higher Education
20 West State Street
P.O. Box 542
Trenton, NJ 08625-0542
Phone: (609) 292-4310
Fax: (609) 292-7225
Website:
www.state.nj.us/highereducation

New Jersey
Higher Education Student
Assistance
P.O. Box 540
Building 4
Quakerbridge Plaza
Trenton, NJ 08625-0540
Phone: (609) 588-3226
Toll-Free: (800) 792-8670
Fax: (609) 588-7389
Website: http://www.hesaa.org/

New Mexico
Higher Education Department
1068 Cerrillos Road
Santa Fe, NM 87505
Phone: (505) 476-6500
Toll-Free: (800) 279-9777
Fax: (505) 476-6511
Email: highered@state.nm.us
Website:
http://hed.state.nm.us/index.asp

New York
New York State Higher Education
Services Corporation
99 Washington Avenue
Albany, NY 12255
Phone: (518) 473-1574
Toll-Free: (888) 697-4372
Fax: (518) 474-2839
Email: webmail@hono.org
Website: http://www.hesc.org/

North Carolina
North Carolina State Education
Assistance Authority
P.O. Box 13663
Research Triangle Park, NC 27709-3663
Toll-Free: (866) 866-2362
Fax: (919) 549-8481
Email: programinformation@cfnc.org
Website: http://www.cfnc.org/

North Dakota
North Dakota University System
North Dakota Student Financial
Assistance Program
Department 215
600 East Boulevard Avenue
Bismarck, ND 58505-0230
Phone: (701) 328-4114
Fax: (701) 328-2961
Email: ndus.office@ndus.nodak.edu
Website: http://www.ndus.edu/

Ohio
Ohio Board of Regents
P.O. Box 182452
Columbus, OH 43218-2452
Phone: (614) 466-7420
Toll-Free: (888) 833-1133
Fax: (614) 752-5903
Email: regents@regents.state.oh.us
http://www.regents.state.oh.us/sgs/

Oklahoma
Oklahoma State Regents for Higher
Education
Suite 200, 655 Research Parkway
Oklahoma City, OK 73104
Phone: (405) 225-9100
Toll-Free: (800) 858-1840
Fax: (405) 225-9230
Email: studentinfo@osrhe.edu
http://www.okhighered.org/

Oregon
Oregon Student Assistance Commission
Suite 100
1500 Valley River Drive
Eugene, OR 97401
Phone: (541) 687-7400
Toll-Free: (800) 452-8807
Fax: (541) 687-7419
Email: public_information@mercury.
osac.state.or.us
http://www.osac.state.or.us/

Oregon
Oregon University System
P.O. Box 3175
Eugene, OR 97403-0175
Phone: (541) 346-5700
Fax: (541) 346-5764
TTY: (541) 346-5741
Website: http://www.ous.edu/

Pennsylvania
Office of Postsecondary Education
333 Market Street
Harrisburg, PA 17126
Phone: (717) 787-5041
Fax: (717) 772-3622
TTY: (717) 783-8445
Website: http://www.pdehighered.state.
pa.us/higher/site/default.asp

Rhode Island
Rhode Island Higher Education
Assistance Authority
560 Jefferson Boulevard
Warwick, RI 02886
Phone: (401) 736-1100
Toll-Free: (800) 922-9855
Fax: (401) 732-3541
Email: info@riheaa.org
Website: http://www.riheaa.org/

Rhode Island
Rhode Island Office of Higher
Education
301 Promenade Street
Providence, RI 02908-5748
Phone: (401) 222-6560
Fax: (401) 222-6111
TTY: (401) 222-1350
Website: http://www.ribghe.org/

South Carolina
South Carolina Commission on
Higher Education
Suite 200, 1333 Main Street
Columbia, SC 29201
Phone: (803) 737-2260
Fax: (803) 737-2297
Website: http://www.che.sc.gov/

South Dakota
South Dakota Board of Regents
Suite 200
306 East Capitol Avenue
Pierre, SD 57501-2545
Phone: (605) 773-3455
Fax: (605) 773-5320
Email: info@ris.sdbor.edu
Website: http://www.ris.sdbor.edu/

Tennessee
Tennessee Higher Education
Commission
Parkway Towers
Suite 1900
404 James Robertson Parkway
Nashville, TN 37243-0830
Phone: (615) 741-3605
Fax: (615) 741-6230
Website: http://www.state.tn.us/thec/

Texas
Texas Higher Education Coordinating
Board
P.O. Box 12788
Austin, TX 78711
Phone: (512) 427-6101
Toll-Free: (800) 242-3062
Fax: (512) 427-6127
Website: http://www.thecb.state.tx.us/

Utah
Utah State Board of Regents
Gateway Center
60 South 400 West
Salt Lake City, UT 84101-1284
Phone. (801) 321-7103
Fax: (801) 321-7199
Website: http://www.utahsbr.edu/

Vermont
Vermont Student Assistance Corporation
P.O. Box 20001
Winooski, VT 05404-2601
Phone: (802) 655-9602
Fax: (802) 654-3765
TTY: (800) 281-3341
Email: info@vsac.org
Website: http://www.vsac.org/

Virginia
State Council of Higher Education
for Virginia
101 North 14th Street
Richmond, VA 23219
Phone: (804) 225-2600
Fax: (804) 225-2604
Website: http://www.schev.edu/

Washington
Washington State Higher Education
Coordinating Board
P.O. Box 43430
917 Lakeridge Way
Olympia, WA 98504-3430
Phone: (360) 753-7800
Fax: (360) 753-7808
Email: info@hecb.wa.gov
Website: http://www.hecb.wa.gov/

West Virginia
West Virginia Higher Education
Policy Commission
1018 Kanawha Boulevard, East
Charleston, WV 25301
Phone: (304) 558-2101
Fax: (304) 558-5719
Website: http://www.hepc.wvnet.edu/

Wisconsin
Wisconsin Higher Educational
Aids Board
131 West Wilson Street, Suite 902
Madison, WI 53703
Phone: (608) 267-2206
Fax: (608) 267-2808
Website: http://heab.state.wi.us/

Wyoming
Wyoming Community College
Commission
Eighth Floor
2020 Carey Avenue
Cheyenne, WY 82002
Phone: (307) 777-7763
Fax: (307) 777-6567
Website: http://www.commission.wcc.edu/

Notes

Appendix Four

Robert Byrd Scholarship Agencies

ALABAMA
State Department of Education
Room 3339, Gordon Persons Building
Montgomery, AL 36130-2101
Telephone: (334) 242-8082
Toll Free: (800) 846-0948
Fax: (334) 353-5714
E-mail: dfoliver@alsde.edu

ALASKA
Alaska Department of Education
801 West 10th Street, Suite 200
Juneau, AK 99801
Telephone: (907) 465-8707
Fax: (907) 465-2989
E-mail: melora_gaber@
eed.state.ak.us

ARIZONA
State Department of Education
1535 West Jefferson Street, Bin #2
Phoenix, AZ 85007
Telephone: (602) 542-3710
Fax: (602) 364-1532
E-mail: jlehman@ade.az.gov

ARKANSAS
Department of Education
4 State Capitol Mall, Room 107A
Little Rock, AR 72201
Telephone: (501) 682-4396
Fax: (501) 682-4886
E-mail: mcrank@arkedu.k12.ar.us

CALIFORNIA
Student Aid Commission
P.O. Box 419026
Rancho Cordova, CA 95741-9026
Telephone: (888) 224-7268
Fax: (916) 526-7968
E-mail: cmistler@csac.ca.gov

COLORADO
State Department of Education
1560 Broadway, Suite 1450
Denver, CO 80202-5149
Telephone: (303) 866-6974
Fax: (303) 866-6647
E-mail: kalber_t@cde.state.co.us

CONNECTICUT
State Department of Education
61 Woodland Street
Hartford, CT 06105
Telephone: (860) 947-1856
Fax: (860) 977-1838
E-mail: jsiegrist@ctdhe.org

DELAWARE
Higher Education Commission
Carvel State Office Building
820 North French Street
Wilmington, DE 19801
Telephone: (302) 577-5240
Fax: (302) 577-6765
E-mail: mlaffey@doe.k12.de.us

DISTRICT OF COLUMBIA
District of Columbia Public Schools
825 North Capitol Street, N.E.
6th Floor, Room 6077
Washington, DC 20002
Telephone: (202) 442-5110
Fax: (202) 442-5303
E-mail: michon.peck@k12.dc.us

FLORIDA
Department of Education
Student Financial Assistance
1940 North Monroe Street, Suite 70
Tallahassee, FL 32303-4759
Telephone: (850) 410-5184
Fax: (850) 488-5966
E-mail: osfa@fldoe.org

GEORGIA
Georgia Department of Education
Atlanta, GA 30334-5001
Telephone: (404) 657-0183
Fax: (404) 657-7096
E-mail: jsearle@doe.k12.ga.us

HAWAII
Department of Education
641 18th Avenue
2nd Floor, Rm. V-201
Honolulu, HI 96816
Telephone: (808) 735-6222
Fax: (808) 733-9890
E-mail: dee_helber@notes.k12.hi.us

HAWAII
Pacific Resources for Education
900 Fort Street
Suite 1300
Honolulu, HI 96813
Telephone: (808) 441-1304
Fax: (808) 441-1385
E-mail: ehrhornk@prel.org

IDAHO
State Board of Education
650 West State Street
Boise, ID 83720-0037
Telephone: (208) 332-1574
Fax: (208) 334-2632
E-mail: dana.kelly@osbe.idaho.gov

ILLINOIS
State Board of Education
1755 Lake Cook Road
Deerfield, IL 60015
Telephone: (847) 948-8500 ext. 2111
(800) 899-4722 ext. 2111
Fax: (847) 831-8549
E-mail: cshields@isac.org

INDIANA
Department of Education
150 West Market Street
Suite 500
Indianapolis, IN 46204
Telephone: (317) 233-1178
Fax: (317) 232-3260
E-mail: yherlin@ssaci.in.gov

IOWA
State Department of Education
200 10th Street
4th Floor
Des Moines, IA 50309
Telephone: (515) 242-3380
Fax: (515) 242-3388
E-mail: brenda.easter@iowa.gov

KANSAS
Kansas State Dept. of Education
120 S.E. Tenth Avenue
Topeka, KS 66612
Telephone: (785) 296-4950
Fax: (785) 296-7933
E-mail: tmiller@ksde.org

KENTUCKY
KHEAA
P.O. Box 798
Frankfort, KY 40602-0798
Telephone: (502) 696-7229
1-800-928-8926, ext. 7229
Fax: (502) 696-7373
E-mail: blane@kheaa.com

LOUISIANA
State Department of Education
P.O. Box 94064
Baton Rouge, LA 70804
Telephone: (225) 342-2098
Fax: (225) 342-3432
E-mail: melissa.hollins@la.gov

MAINE
Department of Education
Financial Authority of Maine
5 Community Drive, P.O. Box 949
Augusta, ME 04332
Toll Free: (800) 228-3734 ext. 230
Fax: (207) 623-0095
Email: croy@famemaine.com

MASSACHUSETTS
State Department of Education
350 Main Street
Malden, MA 02148
Telephone: (781) 338-6304
Fax: (781) 338-6332
E-mail: steixeira@doe.mass.edu

MARYLAND
State Department of Education
200 West Baltimore Street
Baltimore, MD 21201
Telephone: (410) 767-0480
Fax: (410) 333-2275
E-mail: wcappe@msde.state.md.us

MICHIGAN
Department of Education
P.O. Box 30462
Lansing, MI 48909
Telephone: (888) 447-2687 ext. 32435
Fax: (517) 335-5984
E-mail: johnsb@michigan.gov

MINNESOTA
Department of Education
1500 Highway 36 West
Roseville, MN 55113
Telephone: (651) 582-8280
Fax: (651) 582-8291
E-mail: valarie.cochran@state.mn.us

MISSISSIPPI
State Department of Education
P.O. Box 771
Jackson, MS 39205
Telephone: (601) 359-4305
Fax: (601) 359-1247
E-mail: twebster@mde.k12.ms.us

MISSOURI
Elementary and Secondary Education
P.O. Box 480
Jefferson City, MO 65102
Telephone: (573) 751-1191 / 1668
Fax: (573) 526-3580
E-mail: laura.harrison@dese.mo.gov

MONTANA
Office of Public Instruction
P.O. Box 202501
Helena, MT 59620-2501
Telephone: (406) 444-2417
Fax: (406) 444-1373
E-mail: cgneckow@mt.gov

NEBRASKA
Department of Education
301 Centennial Mall South
P.O. Box 94987
Lincoln, NE 68509
Telephone: (402) 471-3240
Fax: (402) 471-0117
E-mail: drice@nde.state.ne.us

NEVADA
State Department of Education
700 East Fifth Street
Carson City, NV 89701
Telephone: (775) 687-9228
Fax: (775) 687-9202
E-mail: wskibinski@doe.nv.gov

NEW HAMPSHIRE
State Department of Education
101 Pleasant Street
Concord, NH 03301
Telephone: (603) 271-6051
Fax: (603) 271-2632
E-mail: mgage@ed.state.nh.us

NEW JERSEY
Department of Education
P.O. Box 500
Trenton, NJ 08625
Telephone: (609) 984-6314
Fax: (609) 292-3142
E-mail: sue.sliker@doe.state.nj.us

NEW MEXICO
Public Education Department
120 South Federal Plaza, Room 206
Santa Fe, NM 87501
Telephone: (505) 827-1421
Fax: (505) 827-1826
E-mail: daniel.benavidez@state.nm.us

NEW YORK
State Education Department
Room 1078EBA
Albany, NY 12234
Telephone: (518) 486-1319
Fax: (518) 486-5346
E-mail: lhall@mail.nysed.gov

NORTH CAROLINA
Department of Public Instruction
Division of Human Resource
Management
Center for Recruitment and Retention
Mail Service Center 6330
Raleigh, NC 27699-6330
Telephone: (919) 807-3375
Fax: (919) 807-3362
E-mail: dholloma@dpi.state.nc.us

NORTH DAKOTA
Department of Public Instruction
600 E. Boulevard Avenue, Department
201
Bismarck, ND 58505
Telephone: (701) 328-2317
Fax: (701) 328-4770
E-mail: hbergland@state.nd.us

OHIO
Department of Education
Center for Students, Families and
Communities
25 South Front Street
2nd Floor
Columbus, OH 43215
Telephone: (614) 644-8861
or (877) 644-6338
Fax: 614-995-7544
E-mail: DL-Byrd_Scholarship@mail.
ode.state.oh.us

OKLAHOMA
State Department of Education
2500 North Lincoln Boulevard
Oklahoma City, OK 73105
Telephone: (405) 521-4311
Fax: (405) 521-6205
E-mail: ramona_paul@sde.state.ok.us

OREGON
Department of Education
Public Service Building
255 Capitol Street, N.E.
Salem, OR 97310
Telephone: (503) 378-3600 ext. 2708
Fax: (503) 378-5156
E-mail: winston.cornwall@state.or.us

PENNSYLVANIA
Department of Education
333 Market Street
Harrisburg, PA 17126-0333
Telephone: (717) 783-6583
Fax: (717) 772-3621
E-mail: dbaker@state.pa.us

RHODE ISLAND
Elementary and Secondary Education
255 Westminster Street
Providence, RI 02903
Telephone: (401) 222-4600 ext. 2194
Fax: (401) 222-2734
E-mail: ride0782@ride.ri.net

SOUTH CAROLINA
State Department of Education
1429 Senate Street
Rutledge Building, Room 1104D
Columbia, SC 29201
Telephone: (803) 734-8116
Fax: (803) 753-1804
E-mail: bcope@sde.state.sc.us

SOUTH DAKOTA
Department of Education
700 Governors Drive
Pierre, SD 57501
Telephone: (605) 773-3727
Fax: (605) 773-6134
E-mail: Mark.Gageby@state.sd.us

TENNESSEE
State Department of Education
404 James Robertson Parkway
Nashville, TN 37243
Telephone: (615) 741-1346 ext. 155
Fax: (615) 741-6101
E-mail: kathystripling@state.tn.us

TEXAS
Education Agency
P.O. Box 12788
Austin, TX 78711
Telephone: (512) 427-6333
(800) 242-3062 ext. 6333
Fax: 512-427-6420
E-mail: scipio.brown@thecb.state.tx.us

UTAH
State Office of Education
250 East 500 South
P.O. Box 144200
Salt Lake City, UT 84114-4200
Telephone: (801) 538-7820
Fax: (801) 538-7769
E-mail: susan.loamanu@schools.
utah.gov

VERMONT
Student Aid Assistance Corporation
VSAC P.O. Box 2000
Winooski, VT 05404
Telephone: (800) 642-3177
Fax: (802) 828-3140
E-mail: lemay@vsac.org

VIRGINIA
State Department of Education
School Counseling Specialist
101 North 14th Street
P.O. Box 2120
Richmond, VA 23218-2120
Telephone: (804) 786-9377
Fax: (804) 786-5466
E-mail: willie.stroble@doe.virginia.gov

WASHINGTON
Superintendent of Public Instruction
P.O. Box 47200
Olympia, WA 98504
Telephone: (360) 725-6100
Fax: (360) 586-3305
E-mail: gpauley@ospi.wednet.edu

WEST VIRGINIA
State Department of Education
1018 Kanawha Boulevard, East, Suite 700
Charleston, WV 25301
Telephone: (304) 558-4618
Fax: (304) 558-4622
E-mail: elmore@hepc.wvnet.edu

WISCONSIN
Department of Public Instruction
125 South Webster Street
P.O. Box 7841
Madison, WI 53707
Telephone: (608) 266-3706
Fax: (608) 266-1965
E-mail: beverly.kniess@dpi.
state.wi.us

WYOMING
Department of Education
2300 Capitol Avenue, 2nd Floor
Cheyenne, WY 82002
Telephone: (307) 777-6265
Fax: (387) 777-6234
E-mail: lpicke@educ.state.wy.us